THE MIND ORGAN

Consciousness Recognized by the Mind Organ during Life, Dream, and Afterdeath

DUKKYU CHOI

Copyright © 2024 by Dukkyu Choi

All rights reserved. This book or any of its portion may not be reproduced or transmitted in any means, electronic or mechanical, including recording, photocopying, or by any information storage and retrieval system, without the prior written permission of the copyright holder except in the case of brief quotations embodied in critical reviews and other noncommercial uses permitted by copyright law.

Printed in the United States of America
Library of Congress Control Number: 2024920313
ISBN: Softcover 979-8-89518-328-1
e-Book 979-8-89518-329-8
Published by: WP Lighthouse
Publication Date: 09/25/2024

To buy a copy of this book, please contact:
WP Lighthouse
Phone: +1-888-668-2459
support@wplighthouse.com
wplighthouse.com

CONTENTS

PREFACE 1

PART 1 MIND AND CONSCIOUSNESS

Chapter 1
What Is the Mind? 5

Chapter 2
Five Sense Consciousnesses 9

Chapter 3
Three Elements of Mind 12

Chapter 4
Storage of Mind Information – Store Consciousness 19

Chapter 5
Thinking and Memorizing 22

Chapter 6
The Epitome of Thinking and Its Contamination 27

Chapter 7
Expanded Meaning of Dharma Boundary 32

Chapter 8
Consciousness and the Brain 36

Chapter 9
Dogs' Mind Organ More Developed than Humans 42

Chapter 10
An Inanimate Being Has a Mind Organ.................................46

Chapter 11
Mindfulness...50

Chapter 12
Four Wisdoms Obtained from Eight Consciousnesses............58

PART 2 CONSCIOUSNESS IN DREAM

Chapter 13
The Mysterious World of Dreams 63

Chapter 14
The Dream That Gives Revelation 69

Chapter 15
Why Is It Difficult to Remember Dreams? 75

Chapter 16
A World of Dream Without Fragrance and Taste 82

Chapter 17
Thoughts and Awareness in Dreams 89

Chapter 18
Life is a Long Dream 94

PART 3 CONSCIOUSNESS AFTER DEATH

Chapter 19
The Unknown World of 'After-Death' 98

Chapter 20
Mechanism of After-Death Consciousness 102

Chapter 21
Reincarnation 108

Chapter 22
Why Don't We Remember Our Previous Lives? 113

Chapter 23
The Driving Force for Reincarnation – Karma 119

PART 4 CONSCIOUSNESS-ONLY THEORY AND DIAMOND SUTRA

Chapter 24
The Diamond Sutra - "Practical Principles on Mind" 124

Chapter 25
Summary of the Consciousness-Only Theory 130

Bibliography.. 138

PREFACE

What is the mind? No one denies the existence of mind. However, no one can accurately explain or define the mind. Consciousness is also the same term as mind. I have tried to discover the mind as well as consciousness on the basis of the Consciousness-Only Theory of Buddhism.

The Consciousness-Only Theory explains about six consciousnesses. The first five consciousnesses are sight, sound, smell, taste, and touch feeling. The five sense consciousnesses are recognized when the five physical organs (eye, ear, nose, tongue, and body (skin)) contact the respective objects (light (color), sound, scent, flavor, and tactile objects). The five organs are subjects to recognize the respective sense consciousnesses, and the five objects are objects to be contacted by the respective sense organs. Eye is an organ of sight, ear is an organ of sound, nose is an organ of smell, tongue is an organ of taste, and body (skin) is an organ of tactile sensation.

The Theory explains that the sixth consciousness is recognized when the subject of the sixth consciousness contacts an object of the sixth consciousness. The Theory defines the subject as organ of mind ("Mind Organ") and the object as information of mind ("Mind Information"). The sixth consciousness is accompanied by mental activities (or mental phenomena) such as feelings and emotions.

The five physical organs belong to a physical body, while the mind organ does not belong to the physical body. The five organs are physical and material organs, while the mind organ is a non-physical and immaterial organ. And, the five objects are material, while the mind information is immaterial. The mind information encompasses all knowledge obtained through learning and experience as well as all consciousnesses arising from the six organs, and all feelings and emotions arising from the sixth consciousness. As the five physical organs belong to a physical body, they do not exist if the body dies. However, the mind organ never dies even if the body dies since it is immaterial and it does not belong to the body.

In addition to the six consciousnesses, the Theory explains about a seventh consciousness (Manas). The mind organ contacts and reads mind informations ceaselessly. When we start to think with mind information A, we think about B from A, C from B, D from C, endlessly. Thus, the seventh consciousness is a continuation of the sixth consciousness, thus, the seventh is called "Thinking Consciousness". Furthermore, the Theory explains about an eighth consciousness (Alaya). The Theory explains that all mind information is stored in the Alaya.

In sleeping, the five sense organs are dormant, while the mind organ still works. Dream is a consciousness which is recognized when the mind organ contacts mind informations during sleep. When awaken, the five sense organs start to work again to generate the respective consciousness.

After death, the five sense organs also die and cannot work any longer. However, the mind organ still works. Even after death, the mind organ contacts mind informations to generate mental activities (or mental phenomena). However, there are no means such as language or letters for a dead person to communicate with a living person.

The mind should be understood as a combined concept of Mind Organ, Mind information, and Mind Activity. Mind is in some way analogous to fire. Fire is easily recognized by flame. However, the flame is a phenomenon of combustion which occurs when a fuel burns, but not fire itself. We have been deluded into thinking that flame is fire. Fire produces flame and smoke by burning a fuel. If the fuel is a dry firewood it will produce white smoke, if the fuel is a heavy oil like bunker-C oil it will produce black smoke, and if the fuel is a good charcoal it will burn without producing hardly any smoke.

Mental activities or mental phenomena are analogous to the smokes which are produced when fuel is burned in a fire. The mental activity will likewise be a function of the mind information; if it is a pleasant information one will feel happiness, but if it is an unpleasant information one will experience an unpleasant or agitated mental state. If fuel is Mind Information and smoke is Mental Activity, fire will be the Mind Organ.

PART 1
MIND AND CONSCIOUSNESS

Chapter 1
What Is the Mind?

Everyone understands the mind and no one denies its existence. However, no one can accurately explain or define the mind. Looking at the dictionary meaning of the mind, Wikipedia describes a cross-section of intelligence and consciousness that is revealed as a complex of thoughts, cognition, memory, emotion, will, and imagination that a person thinks about other people or things. By pointing, all the cognitive processes in the brain are described as the mind. Furthermore, it explains that the mind is a set of cognitive abilities that can be conscious, aware, thinking, judging, and remembering as a characteristic that can be applied to other living things, including humans. If we explain the mind in this way, we find that thoughts, cognitions, memories, emotions, wills, consciousness, perceptions, judgments, etc. are also not easy to explain precisely. The more you define your mind, the more you fall into the labyrinth. To define the mind correctly will be more difficult than to discover the cosmogenesis or to find a planet where there is a life.

The reason we could not have defined these concepts correctly up to now is because we could not figure out the constitution of mind. We have confusingly misused the terms relating to consciousness such as mind, thought, emotion, feeling, desire etc. For instance, when we say "See something with **mind**, but not with eyes," the '**mind**' is the subject of the action. On the other hand, when we say "See your *mind*" (as we do in Korea), the '*mind*' is the object or phenomenon of the master, which abides inside. In other words, the term 'mind' can be a subject or an object or phenomena as the case may be. Although there is a big difference between subject and object, we have misused the term interchangeably from case to case. Nevertheless, the misuse has gained general acceptance because the term is non-material, conceptual or abstract. If mind is a physical object having a shape or a material having a taste or a smell, the mind could have been identified in the field of science. However, as the mind is within the scope of non-material domain, it is not clearly defined with scientific knowledge up to now.

Mind is in some way analogous to fire. Fire is easily recognized by flame. However, the flame is a phenomenon of combustion which occurs when a fuel burns, but not fire itself. Fire cannot be defined as an object or a material. We have been deluded into thinking that flame is fire. Fire produces flame and smoke by burning a fuel. If the fuel is dry firewood it will produce white smoke, if the fuel is a heavy oil like bunker-C oil it will produce black smoke, and if the fuel is a good charcoal it will burn without producing hardly any smoke.

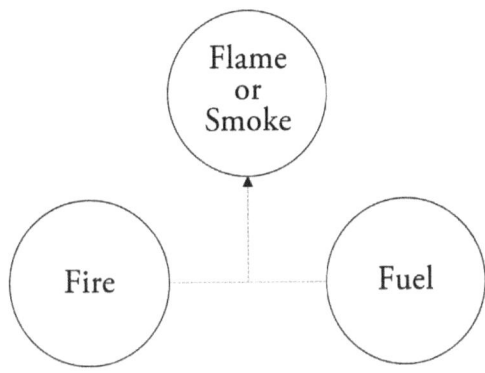

Mental activities or mental phenomena are analogous to the smokes which are produced when fuel is burned in a fire. If we consider the fire which is operating on the fuel to be similar to the subject of mind, then the fuel will be the equivalent of the object of mind which is being operated on by the subject of mind. We can say the subject of mind as "Mind Organ" and the object of mind as "Mind Information (or Mind Material)". The mental activity will likewise be a function of the mind information; if it is pleasant information one will feel happiness, but if it is unpleasant information one will experience an unpleasant or agitated mental state. As "Mind" has been defined in general up to now, we feel it needs to divide into three elements of constitution: Mind Organ, Mind Information, and Mind Activity.

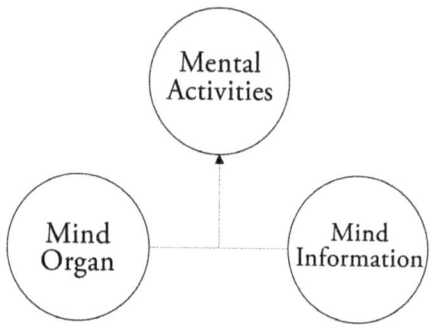

If 'fire-fuel-smoke' is three elements of Fire, 'Mind Organ - Mind Information - Mental Activity' will be three elements of Mind.

Chapter 2
Five Sense Consciousnesses

In order to comprehend thought or mind we have to comprehend consciousness first; and in order to comprehend consciousness, we have to comprehend sense awareness. There are five sense consciousnesses which are common to nearly all members of the animal kingdom. Humans share these capabilities since humans also have an animal body. The five sense consciousnesses we will discuss relate to the five physical organs: eyes, ears, nose, tongue and body (skin). Eye is an organ of sight, ear is an organ of sound, nose is an organ of smell, tongue is an organ of taste, and body (skin) is an organ of tactile sensation. The organ is called "root", a root of sight, a root of sound, and the like.

The eye is an organ which perceives light (color), the ear is an organ which perceives sound, the nose is an organ which perceives scent, the tongue is an organ which perceives flavor, and the skin is an organ which perceives tactile objects. The eye cannot perceive sound or flavor, and the ear cannot perceive light or smell. The five objects are clearly classified depending on the five organs. The five objects are not overlapped. The objects are called "boundaries". Light (color), sound, scent, flavor and tactile objects are also called "five boundaries".

5 organs (5 roots)	eye	ear	nose	tongue	body (skin)
	|	|	|	|	|
5 objects (5 boundaries)	light (color)	noise	scent	flavor	tactile objects
	|	|	|	|	|
5 consciousness	sight	sound	smell	taste	touch

A living animal recognizes objects through the respective five organs, as does a human being. Humans perceive light or color through the eyes, but not all kinds of light can be seen by human eyes. The region of light we can see is just that we call visible rays, those whose wavelength is from about 390 to about 700 or 780 nanometers. We cannot see ultraviolet rays or infrared rays, those which are beyond the wavelengths of the visible spectrum. This does not allow us to say that ultraviolet rays or infrared rays do not exist, however, simply because we cannot see them. Even though human eyes are only able to perceive visible rays, we have utilized the infrared spectrum to create equipment for wireless communication, to warm or cook food, to create motion detectors and home security systems, etc.

We should also note that there are animals which are able to 'see' far beyond the human visual spectrum, with many insects and birds being capable of seeing into the ultraviolet spectrum. Bees are a particularly interesting case of animals which have this extended color vision since they are also peculiarly sensitive to traces of polarization in the light, as von Frisch in Munich found out not long ago; this aids their orientation with respect to the sun in a puzzlingly elaborate way. To a human being, even completely polarized light is indistinguishable from ordinary, non-polarized light.

Sound is very similar to light in that the frequency of sound that we can hear with normal ears is in the range from about 20 Hz to 20,000 Hz, with some humans having the ability to 'hear' sound with frequencies from as low as 12 Hz to as high as 30,000 Hz. As we saw with light, however, there are animals who can hear sounds far outside our normal range of hearing. For instance, elephants and whales hear and communicate using subsonic frequencies; i.e., frequencies which are below the range of human hearing. On the other end of the spectrum, bats, porpoises, shrews and many insects are sensitive to extremely high frequency vibrations ('ultrasound') far beyond the upper limit of human hearing. Many of these animals produce the ultrasound themselves and emit it not only to communicate with each other, but also using it as a sort of 'radar' to detect prey and avoid obstacles. Dogs, elephants, bears, sharks, many insects, etc. have a much better sense of smell than does a human, and the senses of taste and touch are also greatly expanded by other members of the animal kingdom.

Chapter 3
Three Elements of Mind

The attempt to explain the mind as 'mind organ - mind information - mind phenomenon' by comparing the mind to 'fire – fuel - smoke' is based on the Consciousness-Only Theory of Buddhism. As a Buddhist doctrine that the origin of all existence is Consciousness-Only, it is a theory that explains about the principle of creation of mind (consciousness). If a being is in a state without consciousness, that existence would have no meaning as a being. Even from this point of view, the Consciousness-Only Theory can be said to have scientific rationality and legitimacy apart from the doctrine of a religion.

The Consciousness-Only Theory explains the five organs (roots), which are the subjects of the five-sense consciousnesses, and the five boundaries, which are the objects which are contacted by the subjects, respectively. Further, the Theory develops the sixth consciousness which is produced by the mind organ through contacting the mind information.

6 sensory organs:	eye	ear	nose	tongue	body	mind organ
	|	|	|	|	|	|
6 sense objects:	light	noise	scent	flavor	tactile object	mind information
	|	|	|	|	|	|
6 consciousness:	sight	sound	smell	taste	touch	mind consciousness

The Consciousness-Only Theory of Buddhism is the only one that defines the subject that causes consciousness by accessing mind information as Mind Organ in the same way as the five sensory organs (five roots). In any academic field, including medicine or psychology, there is no case where the subject of mind is separately defined from 'mind'. In the Consciousness-Only Theory only, the subject of mind consciousness was named as Mind Organ (Mind Root), and the object of the Mind Organ was named Dharma Boundary (Mind Information or Mind Seed: 6th Boundary). And the Theory explains that the Mind Organ generates a mind consciousness (6th consciousness) by contacting a mind information (mind seed) in the Dharma Boundary. In Buddhism, 'dharma' means Buddha's teachings, but the Dharma Boundary in this book means the objects which are accessed by the Mind Organ to produce a mind consciousness (6th consciousness). In this view, the Dharma Boundary is called Mind Information or Mind Seed.

There is an important difference between the 5 sensory organs and the 6th organ (mind organ). The five organs are part of the physical body and are material organs, whereas the mind organ is a non-material organ. Since the five organs are part of the physical body, they die together when the body dies. So, when the body dies, the 5 sense consciousnesses do not occur. However, the mind organ has nothing to do with the life and death of the body. Even when the body dies, the mind organ does not die, so even after the body dies, the mind organ operates and causes consciousness.

If the mind organ was a material organ, the mind would have been easily identified like the other five organs and therefore would not have been the subject of investigation. Since the 5 sensory organs are material organs, many things have been identified by science. However, the mind organ is a non-material organ, and there is little that has been identified by science. Recently, technologies such as artificial intelligence and big data have been developed to develop robots that can read human thoughts and emotions with intelligence comparable to humans, but the mind organ, a non-material organ, remains a subject of labyrinth.

The existence of the mind organ cannot be denied just because it is a non-material organ and has not been identified. It is like denying the existence of mind or fire. We experience that various minds (actually corresponding to emotions or feelings) arise depending on the situation, but we do not know the subject. It is as if fire meets fuel and produces various flames and smoke, but does not know about fire.

The mind information (Dharma Boundary), which is the object of the mind organ, is a non-material information, but it is a concrete information. My name, age, social security number, birthday, height, weight and so on are also part of the mind information. The multiplication table learned in elementary school or the

Pythagorean theorem learned in middle school ($a^2+b^2=c^2$ in a right triangle: c is the hypotenuse) are also a mind information. The mind information encompasses all knowledge, feelings, and emotions obtained through learning and experience.

When the mind organ contacts a mind information, a consciousness arises. To distinguish this consciousness from the 5 sense consciousnesses, it is also called the 6th or Dharma consciousness or mind consciousness. The 6th consciousness is named because the mind organ is the 6th organ, the Dharma consciousness is named because it occurs from the Dharma boundary, and the mind consciousness is named because it occurs by the mind organ. The 6th consciousness accompanies a mind phenomenon like the 5 sensory consciousnesses. Just as a fire causes various flames and smoke depending on the fuel, the mind organ causes various mind phenomena depending on the mind information it encounters. Mind phenomena correspond to emotions or feelings, such as love, hate, joy, displeasure, jealousy, and envy. The mind phenomena can be easily perceived because everyone has experienced it. However, just as we have mistaken the flame for fire, we have mistaken the mind phenomena for mind itself. Mental phenomena or mental activities (*caittas*) have the same meaning as mind phenomena.

According to the Consciousness-Only Theory, the nature of mind information is classified as *good*, *no-good* and *non-defined*. The mental activities associated with these types of mind information are pleasure, pain, and indifference respectively. When the mind organ works with a *good* mind information, one will experience pleasant feelings; when the mind organ responds to a *no-good* mind information, one will feel pain; and when the mind organ interacts with a *non-defined* type of mind information, one will feel indifference.

Mental activities include all kinds of feelings, moods, emotions etc. The Consciousness-Only Theory explains that there are fifty one mental activities which can be classified as being in six categories: good caittas, vexing passions, secondary vexing passions, indeterminate mental associates, universal caittas and discriminating caittas. These can be seen in Table 1 on the next page.

There are eleven caittas in the good caittas, and these produce pleasant mind states which are experienced as enjoyable and fulfilling experiences.

There are six vexing passions (*klesas*), which are attitudes which lead to frustration and ineffective coping with the situations we encounter. *Klesas* in Sanskrit mean 'seeds of *dukkha*,' and *dukkha* in Sanskrit is frequently translated as pain or suffering, so *klesas* mean 'seeds of pain' or 'seeds of suffering.' This might better be presented as being 'out of joint' such as rolling on a wheel which has its axle off-center so that the ride is very bouncy and uncomfortable. It is being 'out of sync' with the true Reality by living from the false ego. This is the First Noble Truth in Buddhism: the Buddha said 'Life is dukkha.'

We have seen that there are six vexing passions which throw us out of kilter in our living, but there are twenty secondary vexing passions (*upaklesas*) which are more definitive ways in which the vexing passions are expressed in our life.

There are also four mental activities in the indeterminate mental associates which are neither pleasant nor painful within themselves, but which provide a basis for us to respond in either a positive or a negative way. The five universal caittas can likewise be considered as stimuli for either positive or negative reaction, and finally there are five discriminating caittas which can be stepping stones to spiritual growth and harmony.

Table 1: The mental activities (caittas) as described in the Consciousness-Only school of Buddhism

good caittas (11)	belief, sense of shame, sense of integrity, non-covetousness, non-anger, non-delusion, zeal, composure of mind, vigilance, equanimity, harmlessness
vexing passions (klesas) (6)	covetousness, anger, delusion, conceit, doubt, erroneous views

secondary vexing passions (upaklesas) (20)	fury, enmity, concealment (or hypocrisy), vexation, envy, parsimony, deception, duplicity (or fraudulence), harmfulness, pride, shamelessness, non-integrity, agitation (or restlessness), torpid-mindedness, unbelief, indolence, idleness, forgetfulness, distraction, non-discernment
indeterminate mental associates (4)	remorse, drowsiness, reflection, investigation
universal caittas (5)	mental contact, attention (caution), sensation, attention (imagination), volition
discriminating caittas (5)	desire, resolve, memory, meditation, discernment

Chapter 4
Storage of Mind Information – Store Consciousness

Human beings are born, learn to speak and write, and build up an enormous amount of knowledge as they grow. All of this is information gained from experience and learning. Information about the five senses acquired through seeing, hearing, smelling, tasting, and contacting, as well as all emotions and feelings based on them, are all mind information. Where is this information stored? Where is this information stored so that it can be recalled when necessary?

Steven Pinker, professor of psychology at Harvard University, said "The mind is what the brain does; specifically, the brain processes information, and thinking is a kind of computation. The mind is organized into modules or mental organs, each with a specialized design that makes it an expert in one arena of interaction with the world. The modules' basic logic is specified by our genetic program." According to his assertion, our physical organs owe their complex design to the information in the human genome; and so, I believe, do our mental organs.

A Nobel laureate, Francis Crick, OM, FRS, contends that "your joys and your sorrows, your memories and your ambitions, your sense of personal identity and free will, are in fact no more than the behavior of a vast assembly of nerve cells." On the other hand, many cognitive neuroscientists believe that consciousness emerges from the collective activity of those nerve cells throughout the entire brain and is a function of millions or billions of neurons firing together. Francis Crick defines the neuronal requirements for generating consciousness as neuronal correlates of consciousness (NCC), and claims that they involve neurons in the forebrain. However, there is no theoretical basis yet for the mind information obtained through experience and learning to be stored in the brain.

Psychoanalyst Sigmund envisioned the psychic structure as being in three layers: the top or cortex level he called *consciousness*; next was knowledge of which we are not conscious at all times but which can always be called on—this he named the *preconscious*; and the third layer, the largest and most mysterious, he called the *unconscious*. According to Freud's structure of consciousness, the mind information obtained from experience and learning can be seen as being stored in the current consciousness as well as the potential pre-consciousness and the mysterious unconsciousness.

According to the Consciousness-Only Theory, Buddhism establishes Alaya Consciousness as the storehouse of all mind information. It is said that information about all the consciousnesses generated by the 6th organ (mind organ), including the 5 sense consciousnesses, is stored in the Alaya Consciousness. That is why the Alaya Consciousness is also called Storage Consciousness. In addition, the Alaya consciousness is defined as 8th consciousness (7th consciousness will be described later). Alaya consciousness can be seen as an area where mind information, the information of consciousness, is stored, but it is also a non-material concept because it is an area where non-material information is stored. It can be seen as corresponding to the preconscious or unconscious as described by Freud.

As Alaya consciousness is the area where mind information is stored, and the mind organ contacts the mind information in the Dharma boundary so as to produce a 6th consciousness, the Alaya consciousness is the same concept as Dharma boundary (6th boundary) or assembly of mind information. In other words, the 6 organs cause 6 consciousnesses for the respective 6 objects, and the 6 consciousnesses that have arisen become mind information and are stored as they are in the Alaya consciousness. At this point, the Dharma boundary can be identified with one's own Alaya consciousness, but in reality, the Dharma boundary has an extended meaning beyond its own Alaya consciousness (this will be discussed later).

Chapter 5
Thinking and Memorizing

Here is an example: On the way, I met an old school friend after a long time, said hello briefly, and passed by, but I couldn't remember the friend's name at all. Going back to my school days and reviving my memories, finally I found out that his name is 'Thomas Lee'. But my thoughts do not stop there. I continue to think like these: His older brother was 'William Lee', his younger sister was 'Mary Lee', they were all tall, they were good at sports, their parents were blah blah blah, etc. Such thoughts keep going until they are intervened by a new object.

In this example, you would think that the information 'Thomas Lee' had come from somewhere in my head. From a point of view of the Consciousness-Only Theory, the mind organ has found the information of 'Thomas Lee' stored in the Alaya consciousness. This corresponds to memory as finding the information you are looking for among the information stored in the Alaya consciousness. Memorizing is a piece of awareness obtained by contacting a piece of mind information which the subject sought for. And starting with that, more information continues to appear. A series of processes starting with some initial information and continuing to find other information corresponds to thinking (thinking process). Thinking is a series of awareness obtained by contacting a series of mind information one by one continuously.

The process that the mind organ finds the mind information stored in the Alaya consciousness does not stop even for a moment. With this, we say that the mind (thinking process) cannot be still for a moment. We think while walking, think while eating, think while talking, and constantly think while listening to lectures. We liken such a mind (thought) to a monkey climbing a tree. A monkey climbs a tree, grabs one branch, releases it, and grabs another branch, repeating the motions endlessly.

It is said that the average person has about 60,000 thoughts on an average day. One person's mind organ is to find and read 60,000 kinds of mind information a day. In this way, our consciousness moves busily in search of mind information without stopping for a moment, and this characteristic of consciousness is called Nature of Mere-Imagination in the Consciousness-Only Theory. Thus, our consciousness is said to have always a tendency to think and imagine.

In the Consciousness-Only Theory, the process of endlessly finding and reading the mind information stored in the Alaya consciousness is defined as the 7th consciousness, or Manas Consciousness. The Manas consciousness works the same as the 6th consciousness

(Dharma consciousness). However, a series of thoughts (thinking processes) continuing from the mind information stored in the Alaya consciousness are separated from the sixth consciousness and defined as the 7th consciousness. In Manas consciousness, thinking, that is, thinking process, continues, so Manas consciousness is also called thought consciousness or discrimination consciousness. This is because it is differentiated through the thinking process. Through the Manas consciousness, we think dichotomously that this is right and that is wrong, this is good and that is bad, this is long and that is short, this is clean and that is dirty, and so on.

The thinking process which is performed by searching mind information stored in the Alaya consciousness does not arise spontaneously or automatically. Thoughts seem to arise spontaneously, but they never arise spontaneously and must be motivated. Sometimes we talk about something and ask why we are talking about it. For example, there are cases in which friends talk about elephants and ask each other why they started talking about elephants. Then you will know that the story of the elephant originated from a friend's trip to Thailand, the friend's trip to Thailand stemmed from the story of his last year's summer vacation, and the last year's summer vacation stemmed from a special bonus received from his company. In this way, starting with A, thinking about B from A, thinking about C from B, and thinking about D from C is the process of thinking and the process of generating consciousness.

The primary starting point of consciousness or thinking is the five sense consciousnesses. When the five sense organs contact their respective objects the five sense consciousnesses are brought into our awareness, an invoking of the five sense consciousnesses. When an "X" appears in front of your eyes, you think of A from that X, from A to B, from B to C, and from C to D. Then, when you hear "Y" in your ears, you think of Y, think L from Y, think M from L, and think N from M. Then when the scent of "Z" enters your nose, from Z you think P, from P you think Q, and from Q you think R.

The secondary starting point of thought is the 6th consciousness created when the mind organ contacts a mind information in the Dharma boundary. The 6th consciousness occurs when the mind organ reads the mind information. For example, if you can see an object appearing in the distant air, your vision is working. Vision is perceived by the ocular muscles (eyes), the optic nerve, and the brain. Consciousness at this stage is neurophysiological consciousness, sight consciousness (First Consciousness). If it is known that the object is an airplane when it gradually approaches, it is identified as an airplane according to the information already stored by learning or experience. If the aircraft is closer and it is known that it is a national flag, it is also identified as a national flag based on information obtained through learning or experience. Consciousness at this stage is the consciousness at the cognitive or discriminating stage, mind consciousness (Sixth Consciousness) and is recognized by the mind organ.

The 5 sense consciousnesses, the primary starting point of thinking, and the 6th consciousness, the secondary starting point, trigger continuous thinking. The mind information in Alaya is continuously contacted by the mind organ which constitutes a continuous thinking process. The thinking is developed or evolved by contacting new pieces of information one by one. Thinking is not necessarily generated independently but may be generated as a result of earlier processes. Previous information results in a subsequent consciousness; i.e., the previous information becomes a cause of the next consciousness. This characteristic of consciousness is called 'Nature of Dependence on Others' in the Consciousness-Only Theory. This is analogous to causationism, a theory in the Buddhist tradition that every event is the result of a preceding cause. In Buddhism, nothing exists independently—all things exist dependent on each other; this exists due to that, and that exists due to this. The Nature of Dependence on Others in consciousness is a causationism for generating 7th consciousness, thinking process.

Chapter 6
The Epitome of Thinking and Its Contamination

B. Pascal, a French philosopher in the 17th century, said, "Man is a thinking reed." He preached that human beings are nothing more than weak beings like a reed in the vast nature, but that they have greatness that can embrace the universe depending on their thoughts. At the same time, Rene Descartes, a French philosopher, regarded thought as being the fundamental essence of existence for human beings and stated this by declaring *Cogito ergo sum*, "I think, therefore I am." In this way, thoughts represent the origin or greatness of human existence. Thoughts have been the source of human development and evolution. Thought is especially true for human beings since thought has been at the root of our development and evolution. All developments and achievements in science and technology, as well as civilization and culture, have evolved from human thought.

We should also note that thinking is not restricted to human beings. A lesser developed creature such as an ant or an earthworm, as well as more developed animals like chickens or dogs think. Dogs distinguish their master from others, and understand what they are saying and act on it; chickens protect their chicks from an outside threat; ants know how to store their food for winter and earthworms can move to the suitable place to live.

Humans think much more than other animals or living things. This is because an enormous amount of (mind) information is stored in the Alaya consciousness. The reason why humans have so much information compared to other animals is because they know how to use language and letters. As they learn and experience using language and letters, they store a tremendous amount of knowledge, or mind information, in the Alaya consciousness. Then, by constantly contacting the information with the mind organ, thinking continues. Due to the tremendous amount of mind information, human beings have an opportunity to develop a remarkable theory or to devise a fantastic invention during the processing of mind information. We call it research in ordinary language.

In the Consciousness-Only Theory, the 7th consciousness obtained by continuously reading mind information with the mind organ one by one is superior to the 5 sense consciousnesses or the 6th consciousness. It means that thinking, cogitation or intellection in the seventh consciousness surpasses sensation, perception or discrimination in the six consciousnesses. The thought consciousness of 7th, which is a higher level of consciousness that thinks, calculates, and judges, is inevitably superior to 6 consciousnesses, which is a level of consciousness of simple cognition, discrimination, or senses.

The Consciousness-Only Theory says that the Manas consciousness (7th consciousness), which is superior to other 6 consciousnesses, can be contaminated in the thinking cycle since the process of thinking continuously revises and reorganizes the mind information. The Theory says that a pure (mind) information can be contaminated by the self-view in the thinking process of the seventh consciousness. When the thinking process is carried out we hardly obtain a right view because the self-view interjects itself in and disturbs it. The thinking process is self-centered and the pure (mind) information is contaminated with self-view. This is analogous to someone who draws water to one's own mill.

The self-view is again classified into four fundamental defilements (vexing passions): self-delusion, self-belief, self-conceit, and self-love. Self-delusion means lack of understanding. It means ignorance of the true nature of the Atman (the 'inner self' or 'higher self') or individual divine essence, and delusion as to the principle that there is no Atman (egolessness). Self-belief means adhering to the view that Atman exists, erroneously imagining certain dharmas (transitory conditions which cause creation) to be the self when they are not so. Self-conceit means pride; basing itself on the belief in an Atman, it causes the mind to feel superior and lofty. Self-love means a greedy desire for the self; because of its belief in the Atman it develops deep attachments to it. The four vexing passions are from the wrong view that we believe in 'individual ego' and attach to it.

The 7th consciousness is supreme, but it can be contaminated by the defilement of self-view, so in the Diamond Sutra Buddha Shakyamuni teaches to be careful. As long as the self-view is not thrown away, the Sutra teaches that it is impossible to be a Bodhisattva (Buddhist saint). It teaches us not to attach to the self-view because the self-view is a false image with no true self. This is the first teaching of the Sutra.

Professor Daniel Gilbert of Harvard University's Department of Psychology, who is famous for his research on 'emotional prediction (the ability to predict emotional reactions to future events)' as a social psychologist, said that "*People have a tremendous talent for changing their views of events so that they can feel better about them. We're not immediately delighted when our wife runs away with another guy, but in fairly short order most of us start to realize that "she was never really right for me" or that "we didn't have that much in common." Our friends snicker and say that we are rationalizing—as if these conclusions were simply wrong because they are comforting. ..... What matters is that human beings are exceptionally good at discovering them when it is convenient for them to do so.*"

The insight of Buddhism 2500 years ago that the original mind information can be contaminated by the involvement of fundamental defilements such as prejudice, preconception, and delusions of discrimination derived from self-view in the cycle of thought (Manas Consciousness) is an outstanding insight.

Chapter 7
Expanded Meaning of Dharma Boundary

Walking along a crowded street, when you looked back because you had a hunch that somebody was following you, and you found that a friend of yours was actually following you, the hunch would be telepathy, a sixth sense, an ESP or the sixth consciousness. No matter what the name is, nobody can deny its existence. Frederic W. H. Myers, one of the founders of the Society for Psychical Research, was the first person to introduce the term 'telepathy' at the Society's meeting in December 1882. Telepathy, he said, was intended "to cover all cases of impression received at a distance without the normal operation of the recognized sense organs." It should be noted that Myers' definition did not specify that the impressions in question had to emanate from another mind or consciousness. The word telepathy, however, was commonly assumed to imply a supernatural or paranormal connection with some other mind—either that of a living person or that of a disembodied soul.

Telepathy is necessarily related to other 19th century forms of communication from a distance through new and often invisible channels including telegraphy, photography, telephone and gramophone. If disembodied words could be transmitted in an instant across vast distances, why couldn't thoughts and other 'psychic impressions' be transmitted in an analogous manner? Indeed, Sigmund Freud referred explicitly to this analogy when, a few decades later, he speculated that thought-transference might be regarded as 'a psychical counterpart to wireless telegraphy.' Richard Francis Burton, that master of intrusiveness, was the originator of the term that we now call ESP. Richard Burton did not believe in an afterlife but he clearly did believe in a 'sixth sense.'

And even now, over 120 years after the founding of the Society for Psychical Research, the question of whether telepathic communication really exists is still in dispute. On the one hand are the inveterate skeptics. They have repeatedly challenged the validity of studies purporting to have found evidence for ESP, and they have documented many instances in which the results could be attributed to other factors including cheating, fraud, collusion, and insufficient experimental controls. On the other extreme are the credulous enthusiasts: they take it for granted that ESP exists; they believe the apparently supportive research findings; and they vigorously resist any skeptics' attempts to 'explain it all away.' Occupying the middle ground between these two positions are people whose own skeptical need to be convinced is balanced by a genuine open-mindedness.

Their position is represented by a current generation of scientists who seek to investigate ESP and other anomalous experiences without bias or prejudice, using the most valid and defensible methods available. The general consensus of these reviewers is that it is difficult to explain away all of the evidence for extrasensory perception. Although the existence of ESP has not been definitively proved, neither has it been definitively discredited.

Telepathy, extrasensory perception (ESP), and the sixth sense are the same as the sixth organ (mind organ) reading the sixth boundary (mind information) to give rise to the sixth consciousness (consciousness or dharma consciousness).

The mind information which is mainly read by the mind organ is stored in its own Alaya. So, in the previous section (Chapter 4), Alaya was identified with the sixth boundary (Dharma boundary). However, telepathy is not reading the information stored in one's own Alaya, but reading the mind information of others. If so, the sixth boundary must include not only one's own Alaya consciousness, but also the mind information stored in others' Alaya consciousness, and furthermore, the mind information of any other being, such as a soul. Therefore, the sixth boundary, the object of the mind organ, encompasses not only the mind information stored in one's Alaya consciousness, but also the mind information stored in the Araya consciousness of all sentient beings in the universe. In *Yogacarabhumi-sastra*, the Dharma boundary as the sixth object is explained as both one's own objects and others' objects. We believe that the former means the mind information stored in one's own Alaya, and the latter the mind information of others' Alaya which exists in the cosmos.

Chapter 8
Consciousness and the Brain

The mechanism of consciousness in the Consciousness-Only Theory has a structure consisting of eight consciousnesses. The first 5 consciousnesses are sense consciousnesses which are recognized by the respective 5 sense organs. The 6th consciousness is recognized by the sixth organ (mind organ) through contacting the mind information which is stored in the Dharma boundary (Alaya). If the first 5 sense consciousnesses are primary and direct consciousnesses, we can say that the sixth consciousness is secondary and indirect consciousness. The 7th consciousness (Manas) is a repeating or continuing process of the 6th consciousness. In this view, the 7th consciousness is the same as the 6th as secondary and indirect. All mind information is stored in the 8th consciousness (Alaya). Strictly speaking, the 8th consciousness is not a consciousness, but a store house of mind information.

6 sensory organs:	eye	ear	nose	tongue	body	mind organ
	|	|	|	|	|	|
6 sense objects:	light	sound	smell	taste	tactile object	mind information
	|	|	|	|	|	|
6 consciousness:	sight	sound	smell	taste	touch	mind consciousness
	(1st)	(2nd)	(3rd)	(4th)	(5th)	(6th)

7th (Manas): repeating or continuing of the 6th

8th (Alaya): store house of 1st through 7th

1st through 5th: 5 Primary consciousnesses

6th through 8th: 3 Post (Secondary) consciousnesses

There are several characteristics of the 8 consciousness mechanism of the Consciousness-Only Theory. First of all, the 5 sense consciousnesses are recognized by the respective sense organs constituting the body. Thus, when the body dies, the 5 sense consciousnesses do not occur. However, the 6th consciousness is recognized by the mind organ (6th organ) which is a non-material organ independent of the body. Since the mind organ has nothing to do with the life and death of the body, the 6th consciousness arises regardless of the life and death of the body. The next characteristic of the Consciousness-Only Theory is that the 6th organ, even if it is a non-material organ, has a contact object like the five sense organs. Just as the 5 sense organs (eye, ear, nose, tongue, and body (skin)) cause the respective consciousnesses by contacting the respective objects (color (light), sound, smell, flavor, and tactile objects), the mind organ also causes the 6th consciousness by contacting its object (6th object, 6th boundary, Dharma boundary, or mind information). Lastly, the 7th consciousness (Manas) is a repeating or continuing process of the 6th consciousness, and its own object is not defined. The 8th consciousness is not a consciousness, but a store house of mind information. The 8th consciousness does not have its own object.

The 5 sense consciousnesses are primary consciousnesses perceived from external physical objects, and they are called '5 primary consciousnesses'. On the other hand, the 6th, 7th (Manas) and 8th (Alaya) are secondary consciousnesses perceived from the mind information which had been generated by the primary consciousnesses or a store of the mind information, and they are called '3 post (secondary) consciousnesses'.

We believe that the brain thinks. We must acknowledge that many neuroscientists believe that the mind or consciousness comes from the brain, that the brain is the organ which generates them. In fact, most neuroscientists believe that the mind or consciousness is a by-product, or epiphenomenon of the brain; mind vanishes when the brain dies and that is all there is to it. In the medical or neuroscience research literature they have attempted to prove that the brain thinks by researching the changes or phenomena which occur in the brain during the process of thinking.

The scientific hypothesis that the brain is the source of thought or consciousness started to be criticized in Western science during the 19th century. William James, M.D. and Professor of Philosophy pointed out more than a century ago that the evidence for mind/brain correlations may indeed imply that the brain produces mental events, that it has the lesser role of simply releasing or permitting them, or that it merely transmits them as light passes through a prism resulting in a spectrum of colors. In this regard B. Alan Wallace, Ph.D., criticizes that with their bias toward materialism, most cognitive scientists simply assume that the first hypothesis is correct despite the lack of compelling scientific evidence.

The Western scientists who assert that the brain thinks by itself and the mind comes from the brain present experimental and material evidences that the brain is activated during thinking. But Deepak Chopra, M.D., counterclaims that their assertion is a Western perspective based on our bias for solid, tangible things. The Western scientists insist that the brain must be the source of mind because the brain is a visible object, which is like saying that a radio must be the source of music because it is a visible object from which music emerges. However, Deepak Chopra responded that "It may seem significant that the brain is active during thought, but a radio is also active during a broadcast."

The brain, which constitutes part of the body, is related to the five sense consciousnesses. The five sense consciousnesses start from the respective sensory organ, and occur in the nervous system and brain. However, the sixth consciousness or thought is a mental activity by the sixth organ (mind organ). Then the brain has nothing to do with the sixth consciousness or thinking. A representative case proving that the sixth consciousness or thought does not occur in the brain is the near-death experience. Dr. van Lommel, who conducted the Dutch study of near-death experiences, screened 344 patients whose heart had gone into chaotic twitching instead of a normal regular heartbeat in the hospital. Talking to them within days of being revived, van Lommel discovered that anesthesia or medications didn't affect their experience. What he marvels most at, however, are those reports of consciousness in the absence of brain activity. It instantly nullified the theory of materialists that when the brain dies, death follows.

The brain cannot recognize any objects by itself. No color (light), sound, smell, flavor, or touching can be perceived directly by the brain without going through the five physical organs. However, the brain plays a role in controlling each organ or part of the body according to thoughts. As an example, when you think of plums, your mouth immediately salivates. If the brain can think for itself, it should not do the laborious work of secreting saliva just by thinking about plums. In fact, the secretion of saliva in the situation of eating plums is a physiological phenomenon according to the brain's command. The brain, which recognized the actual situation through the tongue, commanded to secrete saliva. However, it is unnecessary and very inefficient to secrete saliva just by thinking. If the brain is an organ that can think for itself, it must know how to judge that it is not a real situation but only an imagination, and then it should not make the salivary glands secrete saliva.

The brain is just a control tower that controls each organ or part of the body according to thoughts or mental phenomena. The mind phenomenon affects the brain, and the brain is influenced by it to give orders to the body. Depending on the state of the mind phenomenon, the brain directly affects the body such as heartbeat, blood pressure change, breathing change, face color change, body trembling phenomenon, and fingertip condition (handwriting condition). Depending on the mind phenomenon that has occurred, the brain releases beneficial substances such as endorphins. It can secrete hormones, and it can also release harmful hormones such as adrenaline. Stress can cause the brain to release glucocorticoids, killing cells in the hippocampus.

Chapter 9
Dogs' Mind Organ More Developed than Humans

Many pet owners will attest to the ability of a dog or cat to know what the owner is thinking. A few minutes before going on a walk, a dog gets excited and restless; on the day when a cat is going to be taken to the vet, it disappears and is nowhere to be found. The scientist who proved this through experimental research is Rupert Sheldrake of British.

Sheldrake, a trained biologist, now turned speculative thinker, to conduct controlled studies to find out if dogs and cats can actually read their owners' minds. One study was very simple: Sheldrake phoned sixty-five veterinarians in the London area and asked them if it was common for cat owners to cancel appointments because their cats had disappeared that day. Sixty-four vets responded that it was very common, and the sixty-fifth had given up making appointments for cats because too many couldn't be located when they were supposed to come in.

Sheldrake decided to perform an experiment using dogs. The fact that a dog gets excited when the time comes to go for a walk means little if the walk is routinely scheduled for the same time every day, or if the dog gets visual cues from its owner that he is preparing to go out. Therefore, Sheldrake placed dogs in outbuildings completely isolated from their owners; he then asked the owner, at randomly selected times, to think about walking their dogs five minutes before going to get them. In the meantime, the dog was being videotaped in its isolated location. Sheldrake found that when their owners started thinking about taking them for a walk, more than half the dogs ran to the door wagging their tails, circling restlessly, and keeping up this behavior until their owners appeared. No dog showed anticipatory behavior, however, when their owners were not thinking about taking them for a walk. This suggests something intriguing, that the bond between a pet and its owner creates a subtle connection at the level of thought.

The above experiment shows that animals can also read human mind (thoughts) directly. How can the dogs read their master's mind? Since the dogs were blocked from the masters by the building, they could not read their master's thoughts through sensory organs such as eyes and nose. If so, we can say that the dogs had read the mind information of their master by their mind organs.

If the experiments had been about human beings instead of cats or dogs we would not have obtained similar results. It seems to us that animals have a more developed mind organ than human beings in certain areas. That's not to say that human beings are inferior to cats or dogs; there's no need to put ourselves down about the experimental results, but we should rather note that a human consciousness is much more complicated than that of cats or dogs. How can dogs have more developed mind organs than humans? Cats and dogs devote themselves to their caretaker. He provides them with food when they are hungry and takes care of them when they get sick. They haven't got the time to concern themselves with other things except their master. To them their master is an absolute being as important as themselves. What they do not tune in with within the awareness of the master's mind could be a major threat and a significant danger to them. The mind organ for reading the master's mind couldn't help being developed.

Humans are more complex. There is no master to go all-in like a dog or cat. And each person is running his or her own cycle of thoughts according to the (mind) information stored in the Alaya. A huge amount of information acquired while learning and experiencing with language and letters as a means is stored in the Alaya. They are turning the cycle of thoughts bound by their own self-view (ego). They are turning the cycle of thoughts so that the thoughts might be contaminated with their vexing passions. They are turning the cycle at an incredibly fast speed compared to animals due to the huge amount of information.

Humans do not show much interest in trying to develop the mind organ. Our concern is only to satisfy the five sense organs of the body. We are forming the cycle of thoughts in accordance with eight mundane concerns consisting of four pairs of priorities: the pursuit of material acquisitions and the avoidance of their loss; the pursuit of stimulus-driven pleasure and the avoidance of discomfort; the pursuit of praise and the avoidance of blame; and the pursuit of good reputation and the avoidance of bad reputation. The eight mundane concerns are to satisfy the five sense organs.

It takes a lot of time for a baby to learn a spoken language. It takes several years for babies to learn it from their parents or brothers or sisters even if it is their native tongue. They have to repeat listening and pronouncing spoken words in order to train their ears. They also have to repeat reading and writing letters to learn written letters and sentences for several years through kindergarten, elementary school, middle school, high school and so on. We might ask, then, why should it be different for the sixth organ, mind organ? Note that we have not tried to train the sixth organ for the entire length of our lifetime. Meditation is the first step to train the sixth organ and develop their performance.

Chapter 10
An Inanimate Being Has a Mind Organ

In the Diamond Sutra of Buddhism, all beings are classified into nine categories, but these are first defined as animate (moving) beings or inanimate (non-moving) beings. There are four species of animate beings: those born from eggs, born from a womb, born from moisture, and born spontaneously. In inanimate beings including plants, there are five species: species with form, species with no form, species having perception, species having no perception, and species neither having perception nor not having perception.

Among the four species of animate beings, all birds and fowls are born from eggs, and turtles, snakes, crocodiles and the like are also born from eggs, all mammals, including humans, are born from the womb, some worms are born from moisture, and the cicada is born spontaneously from cicada larva. In another instance a pupal state is spontaneously changed to another form to give another birth; e.g., a caterpillar to a moth or a butterfly. All of these four species have the mind organ, so they can cause consciousness through the mind organ.

In the five species of inanimate beings, the species with form are beings that have a form, such as a plant or an inanimate object, the species with no form are beings that have no form, such as a soul, the species having perception are beings that has no form but has cognitive abilities, the species having no perception are beings that has neither form nor cognitive abilities, and the final (ninth) species are beings neither having perception nor not having perception. It is not easy to understand all the five species of inanimate beings, but our primary concern is directed to the four species of animate sentient beings, plants and inanimate objects (5th species of inanimate (non-moving) sentient beings).

The four species of animate beings including humans and small creatures as living beings with bodies recognize consciousness through their mind organ. Plants belonging to the species with form (5th species) of inanimate beings have a much lower level of consciousness than that of the four species of animate beings. In religion "Do not kill an animate being" means "Do not kill the four species of animate beings". Plants also have life and consciousness, but they are negligible compared to the four species of animate sentient beings. However, plants also have shapes (bodies) and mind organ that can respond to light, sound, and smell. It has long been known that branches grow along sunlight and growth is stimulated by playing music.

Bernard Grad, a biologist and professor at Mcgill University did experimental work and observed how barleys grow in pots when watered from three different bottles. One water bottle was grasped for 30 minutes and blessed by a naturalist who loves the plants, another by an insane person, and the third one was not grasped by anyone. Each of these three bottles was used to water different pots, with the result that the barley in the naturalist's water grew the biggest, the barley in the nobody's water was second, and the barley in the insane person's water was the smallest.

Another experiment showed different results on cooked rice. Cooked rice was put into two glass bowls. One bowl was attached with labels 'LOVE' and 'THANK YOU,' the other with labels 'HATE' and 'DAD-BLAMED.' A month later, the rice of the former bowl had been changed into well fermented yeast, but the rice of the latter into badly spoiled mold.

Physicists explain these phenomena as properties of microparticles. Heisenberg, a Nobel laureate in physics in Germany, called microparticles 'particles of infinite possibility' and said 'Microparticles have all the information, wisdom and energy in the universe and know everything. So, they are magical particles with all the possibilities that can be realized into anything, such as animals, plants, water and rocks.' Scientists explain that microparticles are mysteriously not affected by distance at all, and that microparticles that have made a connection even once exchange information with each other forever at a speed faster than light, regardless of whether they are right next to them or on the other side of the universe. According to quantum physics, microparticles have infinite possibilities and communicate with all cosmic information.

In modern physics, the above phenomena are the realms of the atomic and subatomic world. However, in mysticism, they are non-ordinary states of consciousness in which the sense world is transcended. Mystics often talk about experiencing higher dimensions in which impressions of different centres of consciousness are integrated into a harmonious whole. A similar situation exists in modern physics where a four-dimensional 'space-time' formalism has been developed which unifies concepts and observations belonging to different categories in the ordinary three-dimensional world. In both fields, the multi-dimensional experiences transcend the sensory world and are therefore almost impossible to express in ordinary language.

In Buddhism, it is said that all sentient beings have Buddha-nature. Not only the four species of animate beings but also the five species of inanimate beings all have Buddha-nature. If explained in the Consciousness-Only Theory, it can be said that plants and inanimate objects have their own mind organ that can read mind information, and consciousness occurs. It can be also said that barley, water, and cooked rice have their own mind organ that can read the different mind information and produce the different phenomena therefrom.

Chapter 11
Mindfulness

As we live, we hear many words directly or indirectly about the mind, and we learn the importance of the non-material world, such as the mind and spirit. We hear such words as 'look at your heart (listen to your heart)', 'everything depends on your mind set', 'true happiness is in your heart', 'open your heart's eyes', 'open the door of your heart', 'everything is created by your mind (一切唯心造)' 'important things cannot be seen with the eyes, but can be seen with the heart', etc., and we regulate our mind or practice mindfulness. It can be said to be the beginning of mindfulness.

Mindfulness is one of the Noble Eightfold Paths of Buddhism. In Buddhism, there are three important Teachings called the Three Dharma Seals, which are "All things (phenomena) are impermanent", "All things have no self (true nature)", and "All things (phenomena) are suffering". Among the Seals, the third Seal ("All things are suffering") is a Teaching that this real world is all suffering, and that the cause of suffering lies in the self-contradiction in the human mind. However, Buddhism teaches a way to escape from the suffering, and that is the Noble Eightfold Paths. The eight Paths are right view, right thought, right speech, right action, right livelihood, right effort, right mindfulness (正念), and right concentration. It teaches that by practicing the Eightfold Paths, one can be freed from suffering.

In the Chinese word of 'right mindfulness (正念)', the first letter (正) means 'right' and the second (念) means 'mindfulness'. The second letter is again a combination of two Chinese letters, 'present (今)' and 'mind (心).' Thus, the right mindfulness is to look at the present mind. In other words, the right mindfulness means to be aware of the present mind. When we analyse 'mind' into 'mind organ, mind information, and mind activity (mental phenomena)', the present mind corresponds to the mind activity (mental phenomena). 'To be aware of the present mind' means 'to be aware of the mind activity (mental phenomena) occurring at the moment'. The mental phenomena, which we call mind, occur as they change from moment to moment according to the mind information encountered. Depending on the mind information, a total of 51 mental phenomena (mental activities) such as happy, sad, good, bad, angry, foolish and the like occur.

The reason why we take care of the mind by looking at the phenomenon of the mind is to avoid living a foolish life led by the phenomenon of the mind. For example, in an unpleasant or angry situation, if the mind phenomenon cannot be awakened, the mind phenomenon leads to behaviors such as swearing or assault. However, it is not easy to recognize that you are angry when you are angry. This is because you are drawn into your anger before you even recognize that you are angry. Anger triggers the next physical action. However, if you become aware of the angry mind phenomenon, the phenomenon will disappear over time. Even if the angry mind phenomenon persists, if you continue to look at it, it will eventually disappear. Of course, there will be a difference in how long it will disappear depending on how angry you are, but it will definitely disappear sometime.

What the mind phenomenon that has occurred must disappear is like Buddha's Teachings, one of the Three Dharma Seals, "All things (phenomena) are impermanent". The Dharma Seal is one of the Buddhist truths that nothing is eternal or permanent. The physical world of all things, including the universe, always repeats the process of being born, staying, being destroyed, and disappearing. It seems solid, but what is born and made is bound to perish someday. It is also the principle of the Dharma Seal for life to repeat the process of birth, old, death, and emptiness. The same is true of the mental phenomena.

There is a Korean or Chinese word '見性' whose meaning is 'seeing into one's true nature', which is synonymous with mindfulness. The meaning of the word expands to 'attaining Buddhahood or achieving enlightenment.' The word has two Chinese letters. The first letter means 'see or look at,' the second 'nature' literally. The second actually is a combination of two letters again, mind (心) and arise or generate (生). Thus, to see into one's true nature is to see the generating mind, the mental activities; i.e., to be aware of it.

In mindfulness, besides being awakened by looking at the mind phenomena, you must also look at the thoughts that arise endlessly. Thought is for the mind organ to read the mind information stored in the Alaya consciousness (store consciousness). It is to turn the cycle of thoughts by constantly reading an infinite amount of mind information. It is said that a person has 60,000 thoughts a day. He continues to think without being aware of what he is thinking. When you become aware of the thoughts that arise, they stop or slow down.

Thinking arises in the Manas consciousness (7th), discernment consciousness. Thoughts that arise do not remain in thoughts, but continue to be discerned. Divided into self-others, good and evil, likes and dislikes, right and wrong, black and white, and so on, they confront while discriminating, and conflict while confronting. So we are demanded not to discriminate. Think, but do not discriminate, be aware of your thoughts and think rightly. Furthermore, it is said to reach the state of the highest happiness, where even thinking and discrimination are cut off, and thoughts and discriminations about all kinds of agony of life and death disappear. The state of mind in such a state is called Nirvana, and it is called the Fourth Dharma Seal.

However, it is not as easy as it seems to be aware of the arising thoughts or mental phenomena. Cognitive scientists claim that humans can only focus their attention on a fixed object for only 2-3 seconds. It is not so easy to become aware of thoughts or mental phenomena. We make an effort to look at the phenomenon of the mind that is happening, but when another light [color] flies in from the side or a different sound is heard, we soon start to think about that light or sound. If awareness is cut off even for a moment, the cycle of thoughts rushes in like a tide through the gap. Since self-awareness is difficult to sustain like this, it tends to end as a momentary phenomenon. In that sense, self-awareness is called extremely short, momentary consciousness.

Several methods are used to sustain awareness. Representative examples include Breathing practice, Vipassana practice, and Zen practice.

The Breathing practice is to be aware of the mental phenomena by concentrating on inhalation and exhalation. Breathing is life itself. Stopping breathing means death of a life. Therefore, breathing has been a very important subject of practice since time immemorial for physical health as well as mental training. We cannot arbitrarily control our autonomic nerves, but we can control them to some extent through breathing. Breathing reflects your mental state. When the mind is peaceful and quiet, the breathing becomes regular and long. However, when negative thoughts such as anger, jealousy, or fear arise, the breathing becomes more coarse and rapid. So, observation of breathing is awareness of the present moment of the mental phenomenon. Observing the breath cuts off other thoughts. You can stop the thought cycle in the Manas (7th). You can be clearly conscious of the part that you passed without consciousness. Therefore, it is said that breathing has both sides of consciousness and unconsciousness at the same time, and observation of breathing becomes a bridge connecting unconsciousness.

Vipassana (*mindfulness meditation*) is the most powerful practice for keeping aware of the mind (mental activities) and body (physical movements) in Hinayana. Vipassana teaches us to be always aware of four objects: body (physical movements), sensation (five senses), mind (mental activities) and dharmas (thinking). Walking on the street we move our legs and arms, but we are not conscious of moving them. We move our legs and arms without thinking about it since such movement has become a kind of unconscious action. Likewise, most of our body movements are performed as habitual actions without conscious awareness of them. It is like a zombie. In philosophy, a zombie is an imaginary being who behaves and acts just like a normal person but has absolutely no conscious life, no sensations, and no feelings. According to the Vipassana practice we have to be aware of every moment of our body. We also have to be aware of sensation which is generated by the five external objects through the five organs. Thirdly, we have to be aware of mental activities (mental phenomena), and finally, we have to be aware of contacting the mind information, dharmas, (thinking). Without being aware of our body, sensation, mind and dharmas, we will be misled by the sensation, mental activities or thinking.

An alternate approach in Mahayana Buddhism is the Zen practice for attaining enlightenment. The name Zen was derived from a Chinese word (禪), Ch'an in Chinese, Zen in Japanese, and Seon in Korean. The Chinese word is a combination of two letters, (視) and (單). The first means 'see' and the second 'only.' The literal meaning of Zen is to see only, thus to see the mind, mental activities. The Zen practice uses a unique means for attaining enlightenment which is called 'koan' (公案). The literal meaning of koan is official correspondence, official statement, public question or the like. In short, koan may be interpreted as an unsolvable question.

One of *koans* is: You can make the sound of two hands clapping. Now what is the sound of one hand clapping? It sounds paradoxical. *Koans* cannot be solved by intellect, rationality, logic or scientific methods. *Koans* cannot be solved in the material world.

Zen practitioners are designed precisely to stop the thought process and thus to make them ready for the non-verbal experience of reality. By concentrating on an unsolvable question the thinking process is stopped, and thus they finally got enlightenment. Enlightenment is to understand the state of mind and to be able to communicate from mind to mind in order to get the right solution.

Chapter 12
Four Wisdoms Obtained from Eight Consciousnesses

Thoughts are important for human beings, but the awareness of stopping thinking and looking at oneself is also important. The awareness is to look at his thoughts and to see the phenomena of his mind arising from the thoughts. It is said that the awareness is like building a dam on flowing water. All our hearts and minds are occupied by the constant flow of water. Whether they flow aimlessly or with a purpose, they immerse themselves in the flowing water, and are swept away by the flowing water. He is losing himself in the endless cycle of thoughts. Whether there is a purpose or not, he is busily turning the cycle of thoughts and burying himself in those thoughts.

Awareness is wisdom or enlightenment that sees reality by stopping thinking. To see reality is to know what is happening here and now. It is through wisdom that you realize the truth. Wisdom is the mental ability to realize the reason of things and process things accurately. Wisdom is a habit or disposition to perform our actions with the highest degree of integrity under any given circumstance. It is a disposition to find the truth coupled with an optimum judgement as to what actions should be taken. So, wisdom is emphasized for humans.

The Consciousness-Only Theory describes the transformation of the Eight Consciousnesses into the Four Wisdoms. The Consciousness-Only Theory explains that four transcendental wisdoms are attained by transformation of the mental attributes of consciousness. The Four Wisdoms are the Perfect Achievement Wisdom, the Profound Contemplation Wisdom, the Universal Equality Wisdom, and the Great Mirror Wisdom. The Perfect Achievement Wisdom is attained by virtue of the transformation of the five sense consciousnesses, the Profound Contemplation Wisdom by the transformation of the sixth, the Universal Equality Wisdom by the transformation of the seventh, and the Great Mirror Wisdom by the transformation of the eighth.

The welfare and happiness of all sentient beings are promoted through the Perfect Achievement Wisdom. The mind associated with this Wisdom manifests itself through the desire to promote the welfare and happiness of all sentient beings in a diversity of consciously-realized actions of the body and the mind. The five sense consciousnesses arise on the basis of our material world consisting of the five objects. The material world is a world governed by the laws of nature; i.e., water always flows to a lower level, the law of gravity applies to all objects, an onion will not produce a rose, and as one sows so shall he reap, etc. Someone with a troubled emotional nature, or pursuing a get-rich-quick scheme, is acting from a lack of the Perfect Achievement Wisdom. Bribery scandals or seeking goods or gifts for free (without compensation) is another act of one who does not find the Wisdom. Accordingly, the Perfect Achievement Wisdom is important in this material world and we can attain it through the right awareness of the five sense consciousnesses. We can bring the sentient beings into a state of being profitable and edified with the Wisdom.

The Profound Contemplation Wisdom is attained by the transformation of the sixth consciousness. With this Wisdom the sixth organ (mind) perceives the sixth objects (mind information) with profound clarity and without hindrance. This Wisdom is not observed in common sentient beings; this is beyond the physical world. The laws of nature do not apply to the world of the sixth consciousness any more. This is the spiritual world where the mind organ experiences wonderful observations. If the Profound Contemplation Wisdom is attained the mind organ can see unseeable objects, hear soundless sounds, smell scentless scents, taste food without flavor, and be free from space and time. This is why it is also called the Profound Observing Wisdom, for it is in this stage that the six transcendent powers which transcend the senses are obtained. One has the ability to see anything at any distance, the ability to hear any sound at any distance, the ability to go anywhere at will and to transform himself or objects at will, the ability to know others' thoughts, the ability to know the former lives of himself and others, and the ability to destroy all evil passions. In this world a stone Buddha can drop tears and a sterile woman can be pregnant. We call it the metaphysical world, but the world is operated by the sixth organ.

The Universal Equality Wisdom is attained by the transformation of the seventh consciousness. The mind associated with this Wisdom sees the identity of all dharmas, and the complete equality between its own self and other sentient beings. This Wisdom is always united with great benevolence, great compassion, etc., and is the special supporting basis for the Profound Contemplation Wisdom. Note that this Wisdom deals with Equality, which is the opposite of discrimination. In the lower levels we habitually discriminate all dharmas in the thinking process; we discriminate dichotomously all dharmas such as good and evil, right and wrong, virtue and vice, black and white, oneself and others, etc., and are always in conflict between them. The Universal Equality Wisdom cannot be obtained as long as the dichotomous discrimination and the conflict continue in the thinking process. By stopping discrimination in our normal thinking cycle we can attain the Wisdom and at last realize that all sentient beings including myself are equal. In the world of this Wisdom, there is no discrimination between good and evil, right and wrong, virtue and vice, black and white, oneself and others, etc. It is ALL right. The saying that sentient beings are Buddhas and Buddhas are sentient beings is something that can be said by those who have stopped discriminating and have realized the Universal Equality Wisdom.

The Great Mirror Wisdom is attained by the transformation of the eighth consciousness (Alaya). It is the wisdom to see the reality as it is without any delusions of defilement occurring as all the mental information stored in the Alaya consciousness is destroyed. It is the wisdom to see the true nature of all things as they really are, just as a large mirror reflects things as they really are. A mirror reflects the reality as it is. However, when objects or ideas pass through our minds, they do not reflect reality, but instead reflect contaminated objects or ideas stained with prejudice, preconception, and delusions of discrimination. When all contaminated information dissipates, however, all delusion and agony will disappear and the Wisdom will be attained, and at last we see the reality through the Wisdom. It is said that it is the wisdom that only enlightened saints can enjoy.

In the stage of the Perfect Achievement Wisdom, a mountain is a mountain and a river is a river. In the Profound Contemplation Wisdom, a mountain is not a mountain and a river is not a river. Getting up to the Universal Equality Wisdom, a mountain is a river and a river is a mountain. The Great Mirror Wisdom sees again that a mountain is a mountain and a river is a river. However, in the first stage, the mountain and river are contaminated with personal views and personal thoughts. In the last stage of the Great Mirror Wisdom, the mountain and river are reflected in reality as they are, without being discriminated and contaminated.

PART 2
CONSCIOUSNESS IN DREAM

Chapter 13
The Mysterious World of Dreams

We spend about one third of our life sleeping. Sleep is very important for physical as well as mental health. Freud said that sleep is an active psychological process as a state of consciousness with its own laws, breaking away from the conventional passive viewpoint that sleep is driven by instinctive desire. Freud said that sleep is due to periodic biological demands and has its own internally generated rhythm, but motor and sensory functions are lost. Sleep is important from the physical aspect, that is, from the medical or physiological aspect, but from the conscious aspect, the dreams that occur during sleep are important.

We dream while we sleep. To dream is to perceive something. The senses of the body stop for a while because the five sense organs do not function, but we see, hear, and recognize something in the dream. On the other hand, we are aware of something, but while we are dreaming, we are mostly unaware that we are dreaming, and accept the dream situation as if it were a solid reality. That's why we scream and break out in a cold sweat while dreaming. Only when we wake up we escape from the dreams and return to the real, physical world.

The roots of modern scientific thought about dreams can also be found in ancient times. Aristotle proclaimed that far from being a product of divine origin, "dreaming is thinking while asleep." The Upanishads, philosophical treatises written in India between 900 and 500 B.C., proposed that it is the dreamer himself who creates horses, chariots, and other objects appearing in the dream world, and that dream objects were expressions of the dreamer's inner desires.

Published in 1900, Freud's *The Interpretation of Dreams* argued that dreams spring from subconscious wishes (primarily sexual and aggressive desires, which Freud called libidinal drive) that the censoring ego normally suppressed in waking hours. Dreams are symbolic, jumbled stories full of visual images that give the impression that desires and fears are actually being expressed. Freud described dream interpretation as "the royal road to understanding the unconscious activities of the mind."

Carl Jung, who was once one-time protege of Freud, broke up with him due to different views on dreams. In addition to meaning that could be extracted based on each individual's personal experience, Jung proposed that there was another level of meaning in dreams. In fact, he believed the most important dreams we have are the products of what he called the 'collective unconscious,' which reflects the inherited experiential record of the human species. As human anatomy bears telltale signs of its evolutionary past, such as vestiges of a tailbone in the human fetus, so Jung theorized that the mind "can no more be a product without history than is the body in which it exists." He argued that the collective unconscious was expressed through archetypes that appear not only in dreams but throughout history in the content of myths, fairy tales, and religious ceremony. Archetypal dreams are linked with strong emotions and occur more often around times of crisis or transitions in our lives, Jung contended.

The dream, which had been researched within the perspective of psychoanalysis, entered upon a new phase in the perspective of neurophysiology in the 1950s when rapid eye movement (REM - sleeper's eyes dart back and forth beneath closed lids) during sleep was proved. Some define it narrowly as the creation of hallucinatory narratives complete with characters and a discernable plotline that occurs primarily during that period of rest known as REM sleep, while at the other end of the spectrum are researchers who classify any mental activity that occurs during any stage of sleep as dreaming.

In the 1960s, studies on the neurophysiology of dreams centered on EEG (electroencephalogram) or

REM were conducted, and Freud and Jung's theories on dreams were finally rejected. At that time, scholars argued that the reason why the judgment ability to recognize the fact that one is dreaming and the ability to accurately remember dreams is limited is because the neuromodulators necessary for the function are insufficient until waking up. Furthermore, Jung's collective unconscious and archetypal symbols were also regarded as a kind of religious concept rather than a scientific concept.

Humanity, who has believed that the brain thinks, believes that dreams are also dreamed by the brain. During dreaming, rapid eye movements occur, and these movements are caused by the brain's command, so it is said that the brain is dreaming. Science has also revealed that the limbic system is the region most activated during sleep, when dreaming is at its peak. The limbic system is the region that produces memories and behaviors that are loaded with emotions. Thus, the memories that the brain preferentially selects to weave into a dream plot are usually called emotionally charged memories. It is a theory believed by scientists today that more than 100 trillion neurons and synapses form very diverse neural circuits, providing all information and creating dreams and stories at the same time.

According to the Consciousness-Only Theory, a dream is for the mind organ to read the mind information stored in Alaya. Consciousness occurs when the 6 sense organs come in contact with each object (6 boundaries). During sleep, the five sense organs temporarily stop functioning, but the mind organ does not stop functioning and it contacts the mind information stored in the Alaya. As a result, consciousness to see or hear something occurs. The mind organ reads not only the information stored in one's own Alaya, but also the information stored in others' Alaya. It reads not only the information of living people of the physical world, but also the information of all beings of the spirit world, such as ancestral spirits and guardian spirits.

When we close our eyes and think about the Statue of Liberty we can envision the Statue in our mind. Although we do not see the Statue with our eyes, the image appears in our mind. The imagery is perceived by the mind organ which has contacted the mind information stored in Alaya regarding the Statue. When we close our eyes silently and recall the voice of our late mother or father, we can hear the voice. Although we do not hear the voice with our ears, we can remember the voice. The sound imagery is perceived by the mind organ which has contacted the mind information regarding the voice as stored in Alaya. This imagination of artificially stopping the function of the five sense organs is the same as the principle of a dream in which the function of the sense organs is stopped during sleep.

Unlike the reality of contacting and recognizing the outer boundaries such as color (light), sound, flavor, taste, and tactile objects with the respective sense organ, the dream of contacting and recognizing mind information purely with the mind organ is another aspect of our lives. *Insights into the unconscious as presented in dreams are glimpses into a world of Absolute knowledge, and the unconsciousness which is transpersonal is connected to the Cosmic Mind and functions to communicate with the sea of information in the multidimensional world.* A dream is an expression of unconsciousness, and that unconsciousness starts from the world of Absolute knowledge. The world of dreams is fantastic, but much of it remains a mysterious realm undiscovered by science.

Chapter 14
The Dream That Gives Revelation

The Russian chemist, Dmitri Mendeleev, had been working for years in an effort to discover a way of classifying the elements according to their atomic weights. One night in 1869 the chemist fell into bed exhausted after devoting many long hours in an attempt to solve the problem. Later that night he "saw in a dream a table where all the elements fell into place as required." Upon awakening he immediately wrote down the table just as he remembered it on a piece of paper. Amazingly, Mendeleev reported, "Only in one place did a correction later seem necessary." Thus the Periodic Table of the Elements, a fundamental discovery of modern chemistry, was first brought forth in a dream.

One morning in May 1965, Paul McCartney dreamed of a string ensemble playing. The dream was so vivid that even after waking up, the beautiful melody lingered in my mind. McCartney immediately got up and played the melody he had heard on the piano. Since he had heard the melody in a dream, he thought it must be a song he had heard somewhere before. Thus composed, "Yesterday" became one of the most played songs on American radio for decades. McCartney said that the song was "the most perfect song" he had ever written, and that he was very lucky to have had such a special dream.

At the time of his invention, Elias Howe, who invented the sewing machine, was struggling with the problem of securing the needle to the machine so that the thread could pass through it easily. Howe, who could not solve this problem in reality, got the solution in a dream. In the dream, barbarian warriors who painted his face surrounded him and tried to kill him. As he was led by barbarian warriors, he saw the spears they were holding. At the tip of the pointed spear was a slender hole in the shape of an eye. Waking from the dream, Howe realized that the needle for the sewing machine had to be pierced with the pointy end of the needle, imitating the spear he had seen in the dream. That way he was able to complete a sewing machine.

Even if it is not the story of famous people, we may have heard or experienced a story of receiving a revelation from a dream and solving a problem we are facing. Dreams, recognized by the mind organ during sleep, give us special revelation in solving the problems we face in the real world. Everyone has to sleep, and since the mind organ works during sleep to dream, anyone can receive revelation. So, who receives such revelations in dreams?

In order to receive a special revelation in a dream, there must be an earnest wish or longing along with ceaseless efforts in the real world to the extent that the mind organ can work. It must be accompanied by concentration and effort to aspire to a solution to a particular problem. It should be as earnest as a mother's heart praying for the safety of her son who went to the battlefield. Examples of scientists, artists, or inventors receiving revelations from their dreams tell us how much they struggled and longed for a solution. The format may be different for each religion, but there are also stories of experiences of receiving a revelation from a dream after earnest prayer. If you look back on what problems you have been struggling to solve in the real world, and if so, how much effort and desire you put into solving them, you will know for yourself what revelations you received from your dreams.

The next thing dreams reveal to us is about our important affairs of life. What is important to us in this physical world, the material world, is the physical body, that is, life. In the material world, nothing is more important than the body because everything ends when the body dies. The birth of a new life or the destruction of one life is the most important event, and even if it is not life-and-death, an upcoming disease or a physical accident such as a traffic accident is also a major event.

There is nothing more auspicious than the birth of a new life. Precognitive dream about the birth of a child is a dream to inform the birth of a new life. People nearing death often dream of the grim reaper trying to take them away. Coming diseases can be prevented from the revelation of a dream, and a cure for an existing disease can be obtained from a dream. A traffic accident that will happen can be prevented in advance by the revelation of a dream. The mind organ finds the mind information that corresponds to these important events and gives revelation. At this time, the mind organ is connected to the ancestral spirit or guardian spirit and exchanges necessary information. There is no way that the mind organs of ancestors or guardians who transcend time and space are unaware of important events that will happen to descendants or believers. Even if it is not such a major event, dreams that give revelations can appear every night according to the desire even for trivial matters of daily life.

Dreams are almost always perceived visually. Then, it is recognized as auditory information such as voice. In addition, it is also recognized by physical contact. Dreams like wet dreams that can be dreamed by physical contact with the opposite sex fall into this category. In dreams, there is little awareness of smell (scent) or flavor (taste). When we dream of eating something, we rarely recognize the smell or taste in the dream.

Dreams are mostly non-directive. What the dream wants to convey cannot be conveyed as in the real world. Most dreams appear symbolically or metaphorically and have connotative meanings. But not all dreams are metaphorical. Mendeleev's dream of the Periodic Table of Elements or McCartney's dream of 'Yesterday' is a straightforward dream.

Most dreams are expressed metaphorically by visual information. Since it cannot be explained at length through words or text, it appears as a few slides with symbolic meaning. In waking life, the mind information stored in the Alaya is quickly and logically read, but in most dreams, it is not logical and inconsistent because the activated mind information is intermittently contacted by the mind organ in the dream. If the cycle of thoughts at awakening is a continuous video, the scene appearing in a dream is like an intermittent slide turning over one by one.

Western scientists explain the illogical nature of dreams by relating them to physical phenomena in the brain. Because the portions of the brain that normally order our thinking are off-line, what we're experiencing in a dream state can seem to be a hallucinatory world, much like what a schizophrenic experiences in waking consciousness. In fact, brain-imaging studies show that the functional anatomy of dreaming is almost identical to that of schizophrenic psychosis with the major difference being that the visuospatial system is most highly charged for dreamers, while for schizophrenics the audioverbal system is activated. According to a paper published by Allan Hobson and his colleague David Kahn at Harvard, the story that occurs during dreaming may actually be an example of chaos theory at work in the brain. Chaos theory emerged in the 1970s is a new way for physicists, mathematicians, biologists, and other scientists to comprehend the patterns of order that exist within what appears to be disorder.

Due to the metaphorical expression or illogicality of dream, people did not understand the meaning of dreams, and as a result, they began to study how to interpret dreams. The earliest record of dreams comes from Mesopotamia, where clay tablets recounting the adventures of the legendary hero Gilgamesh included accounts of dreams and how to interpret their symbolic and metaphorical imagery. It is believed that texts had been written on how to decipher the meaning of dreams by about 1000 B.C. in both India and China. However, a dream can be most accurately interpreted by the dreamer. This is because the dreamer knows best the circumstances and feelings of the dream at that time. Although pig dreams are known as good dreams in the oriental, they are not all good dreams. It's not a bad thing just because it's a nightmare or a bad dream. If it's a good dream, you can expect good results, but even if it's a bad dream, you can have a period of time to prepare for the upcoming event. There are no bad dreams. We are just ignorant and oblivious to the dream.

Chapter 15
Why Is It Difficult to Remember Dreams?

It is said that people dream every night. People who say they don't dream don't remember their dreams, but in reality, they dream every night. On average, it is said that they have more than 5 dreams per night. However, among them, the dreams they remember are said to be about once or twice a week. Given the fact that we dream every night, we do not remember most of our dreams. There are cases in which we have a dream but do not remember it at all, there are cases where we have dreamed something but do not remember it well, and there are cases where we forget the fact that we had a dream and then remember the dream of the previous night because it is triggered by something during awakened. Of course, a very clear postmonition or a terrifying nightmare that makes you scream may not be forgotten for the rest of your life.

It is said that an average person typically remembers his or her dream only once or twice a week. Given the fact that we all dream every night, that leaves at least ninety-five percent of our dreams forgotten. Hobson or McCarley argued that the sense of judgement we need to recognize that we're dreaming, and the ability to remember exactly what we dreamed, are limited because the two neuromodulators needed for those functions are in short supply until we awaken. Standard memory theory explains much of what is remembered of dreams and what is not, which aspects of dream content are more readily recalled and which aspects are not, and so on. But these explanations do not answer the basic question of why it should be that dreams are so difficult to remember.

A dream is a consciousness that appears for a while by reading the mind information with the mind organ during sleep and then disappears. If the consciousness during dream conveys a message that is clear enough to be remembered again, it can be easily remembered even after waking up, but if not, a lot of mind information will be read for a short period of dream and then disappear without being imprinted.

The process in which the mind organ recognizes the mind information in a dream is similar to the process in which the mind organ recognizes the mind information in the reality at the time of awakening or the process in which the five sense organs recognize respective object (boundary) - color (light), sound, smell, flavor (taste), and tactile object (touch). In the state of awakening during the day, the five sense organs (physical or material organs) and the mind organ (6th or immaterial organ) are active. We recognize the five sense consciousnesses from the five external objects through the five sense organs, and the five sense consciousnesses become the basis, and the mind organ contacts the mind information stored in the Alaya to cause the 6th consciousness. the 6th Consciousness continues incessantly, turning the cycle of thoughts, which is called the 7th consciousness (Manas).

Let's consider the recall of dreams from the perspective of consciousness. Consider consciousness during the waking hours when the six sense organs work busily during our whole waking experience. Suppose that we walked along the streets in New York all day. How many things would we remember from the myriad of things which we encountered from the time of leaving our home in the morning to when we come back home in the evening? Consider all of the buildings, shops, trees, pedestrians, cars, bikes, traffic signals, signboards, and all of the other things, and consider all of the sounds which we heard. In spite of, or maybe because of the sensory overload which we encounter during our day to day experiences we only remember a few things that were either very impressive or that caused some concern. It is also similar in our daily work life. Although we go to work every day and do many things and come back home in the evening, it is not easy to remember all the tasks that we performed or participated in during a given day. The tasks done yesterday are more difficult to remember than those done today, and those done a week ago are becoming far removed from our memory. If what we have experienced is a disastrous traffic accident or a chance meeting with a close friend of ten years ago, such things will be easily recalled in our memory for a very long time.

The same goes for dreams. During the night, the mind organ dreams by contacting the mind information stored in his own Alaya, other people's Alaya, or the Alaya of ancestors or guardian spirits. The mind organ arouses consciousness by seeing, hearing, and contacting something through visual or auditory information. Because the body is sleeping, the mind organ is not in a clear state of awakening like when it is awakened during waking life. Moreover, because dreams are like a series of slides that are neither logical nor coherent, they pass without being sufficiently imprinted to be remembered. A scene that can be imprinted in a bright state of the mind organ can remain in the memory for a long time.

A method for recalling dreams is to try to recall them every morning when we awaken from sleep. Before getting out of the bed, recall dreams and think about what messages they may be delivering. It is also a good way to remember dreams by jotting down the dreams that come to mind. Because that moment is the best time to remember your dream.

Although each person's habits are different, usually going to the bathroom and reading the newspaper delivered to the front door, drinking a cup of tea, turning on the TV to watch the morning news, going out for a walk, etc. we start our daily life. Although these routines are routine, they are the process by which new information about color, sound, smell, flavor, and touch comes in through the respective sense organs. The dream we had last night is pushed away by this new information and gradually fades away from our memory. What happened today is best remembered today. As time passes, it fades from memory. The same goes for dreams. It is best to remember a dream when we wake up immediately after it has occurred.

If we see or feel something during our daily routine which reminds us of last night's dream, we are spontaneously reminded of fragments of the dream. For example, we may recall a dream related to cars the moment we pass by the scene of a car crash. This is a kind of memory technique by association. A dream researcher, Braun maintains that this phenomenon occurs because the dream content is actually encoded in the brain.

The memory of a dream is a reproduction of consciousness. The consciousness generated in the dream becomes the mind information and is stored in the Alaya. The memory of dreams is the rereading of the mind information stored in the Alaya. If the mind information is not so distinct that it is not imprinted, it will not be easy to remember; if it is imprinted, then it will not be easily forgotten. If the mind information is stored in the Alaya without distinction, you will remember the dream when you come across something related to the dream. In other words, the forgotten dream is remembered by some motive. And the dream of one scene that I remembered is motivated again and I can remember the previous scene. This is the 'memory technique for dreams in reverse order' that LaBerge describes as remembering dreams. This technique can be applied to the thinking process in waking hours. We can trace the present thinking content A as A was from B, B was from C, C was from D, and so on. The production or reproduction of consciousness is not a spontaneous occurrence but is rather a result of causes and conditions. This is one Nature of Consciousness in the Consciousness-Only theory so called 'the Nature of Dependence on Others'.

Now that we have considered how one might better recall dreams upon awakening, we should note that it is not necessary to force oneself to remember a dream which is difficult to recall. Trying to remember a 'lost' dream is similar to trying to remember what one has done in daily life. Although it is not unimportant to look back and recall what one has done in daily life, the more important thing is not to let go of the consciousness of every moment, the consciousness of the 'now' moment. We perceive a lot of information from external or internal objects and act on the perceived consciousnesses in daily life even though we are not aware of most of them. When we perceive a mind information, a consciousness is generated and the brain and nervous system respond to the consciousness even though the mind organ is not aware of the consciousness or the brain's response. If we practice to remain aware of our consciousness in daily life, we will likewise be aware of the consciousness during our dreams and will be better able to recall them. That way, you won't just let go of necessary and important dreams.

Chapter 16
A World of Dream Without Fragrance and Taste

We perceive dreams mostly with visual imagery. The investigations of dream content from the 1890s and later consistently showed that nearly every dream contains visual imagery, while slightly more than half contain some auditory component. Among other sensations, touch or feelings of movement are present in less than 15 percent of dreams, while taste or smell rarely figures into dream experience at all.

The mind information stored in the Alaya consists of visual information, auditory information, olfactory information, taste information, tactile information, and thought information (consciousness information). Visual information occupies the largest amount of the mind information. A huge amount of information comes in through eyes, followed by auditory information or thought information. Visual information is so much more than other sensory information that one-third of the brain is allocated to processing visual information. The eye is superior to other sensory organs in terms of sensory information, to the extent that it can be said that one picture is worth a thousand words. Olfactory information, taste information, and tactile information are very limited compared to visual or auditory information. Since olfactory and gustatory information is much smaller than other information in terms of quantity, it seems that we hardly experience scent and taste even in dreams.

According to the Buddhist view of the universe, there is a world without fragrance and taste. It is a world called the Form Realm. It is said that there is no fragrance and taste in the Form Realm, but if fragrance and taste are not experienced in dreams, it can be said that the Form Realm of Buddhism and the world in dreams have something in common.

In Buddhism, the universe is divided into three Realms: Desire Realm, Form Realm, and Formless Realm. Since the degree of greed (desire) is closely related to consciousness, the view of the universe in the three Realms can be said to be a view of the universe divided according to consciousness. The Desire Realm again consists of 18 subrealms, the Form Realm consists of 14 subrealms because there is no scent and taste, and the Formless Realm consists of 3 subrealms with only consciousness (6th consciousness).

The desire of the Desire Realm consists of three basic desires of voracity, sleep, and lust, as well as five sensory desires for the five external boundaries. The world dominated by these eight desires is the Desire Realm. In the Desire Realm, the six sensory organs, the six sensory objects, and the six senses (consciousnesses) arising from each of these form eighteen subrealms.

Eighteen Subrealms in the Desire Realm

(Sense Organ)	Eye	Ear	Nose	Tongue	Body	Mind Organ
	|	|	|	|	|	|
(Object)	Light (Color)	Noise	Scent	Flavor	Tactile Object	Mind Information
	|	|	|	|	|	|
(Consciousness)	Sight	Sound	Smell	Taste	Touch	Sixth Consciousness

In another aspect, the Desire Realm is divided into six Worlds: Human World, Animal World, Hell World, Hungry Ghost World, Warlike (Asura) World, and Heaven World. It is said that sentient beings repeat reincarnation in these six Worlds. It is said that if you commit good karma during life, you will be reborn in the Human World, Warlike World, or Heaven World, and if you commit bad karma, you will be reborn in the Animal World, Hell World, or Hungry Ghost World.

The Human World is not difficult to understand as the world we live in. It is a world where there are physical bodies on which five sense organs are attached, and there is a mind organ that is a non-material sense organ, and the 6th consciousness arises from it. Since the 7th consciousness (Manas) is an extension of the 6th consciousness, it does not constitute a separate subrealm. The 8th consciousness (Alaya) does not also constitute a separate subrealm as the mind information stored in the Alaya falls into the mind information of the 6th boundary. The Animal World is not difficult to understand because the World also lives with us and is a world in which animals live. However, the Animal World, where the amount of the mind information stored in the Alaya of animals is extremely limited due to the lack of language and text, is a much simpler world than the Human World from the point of view of consciousness.

The Hell World is a world where those who have committed bad karma enter after death. The Hell World is a realm that cannot be easily explained. However, the World can be easily understood if explained in relation to consciousness, especially consciousness in dreams. When we dream of snakes swarming or vipers rushing to bite us, we run away or scream in terror. You may even break out in a cold sweat. In a dream, even though the poison does not spread through the body of those bitten by a poisonous snake, they do not recognize that it is a dream and accept it as reality, so they actually face a time of fear. The fear in dreams is like the Hell World. However, Buddhism teaches that the Hell World belongs to the Desire Realm, and that the Desire World has a body equipped with five sense organs. It does not fit logic to say that there is a body suffering when there is no body because it is already dead. However, the body in the Desire World includes not only a physical body, but also a virtual body (or 'body of consciousness') like in a dream. The body that suffers in a dream is a virtual body. Even though we are not actually bitten by a poisonous snake, our virtual body suffers just like the real one. Even if the physical body dies, as long as desire remains, one cannot escape the Desire World where the virtual body exists.

The Hungry Ghost World is also a world where those who have committed evil karma enter after death. The Hungry Ghost world is a world where the stomach is the size of a huge mountain but the throat is like a needle hole, so no matter how much they eat, they are always hungry. That's why it's a world where they fight to eat a just little more. After all, even if the physical body is dead, the desire cannot be extinguished, so it is a world where a virtual body exists like in a dream.

The Asura (Warlike World) is a world that likes to constantly wage war and creates a world like mayhem. Although they have both sides of good and evil, they are regarded as good gods (Aditya) rather than evil gods (Danava) in terms of protecting Buddhism and realizing justice.

The Heaven World is a world where we can go only when we commit good karma, and it corresponds to a paradise or a heaven. Even if we are born in the Heaven World, our greed (desire) still exists and we have a virtual body. As long as a (virtual) body exists, it must someday reach the end of its lifespan, perish, and be reborn in one of the six Worlds.

The Form Realm is a world in which fine forms are still left, although greed (desire) is destroyed by cultivating meditation (samatha). In the early Buddhist treatise, *Abhidharmakosha*, it is said that there is no fragrance and taste in the Form Realm. Therefore, the Form Realm consists of 14 subrealms.

Fourteen Subrealms in the Form Realm

(Sense Organ)	Eye	Ear	Nose	Tongue	Body	Mind
	|	|	|	|	|	|
(Object)	Light (Color)	Noise	~~Scent~~	~~Flavor~~	Tactile Object	Mind Information
	|	|	†	†	|	|
(Consciousness)	Sight	Sound	~~Smell~~	~~Taste~~	Touch	Sixth Consciousness

In the Form Realm, the desire has been mostly extinguished, but the Form (body: vertual body) still exists, so the six organs still exist. However, since there is no flavor and taste among the external objects, the smell consciousness and taste consciousness do not occur. Therefore, the Form Realm does not have four subrealms of flavor, taste, flavor consciousness, and taste consciousness, so all of them consist of 14 subrealms. The Form Realm is similar to the dream world without fragrance and taste. Experiencing the dream world without fragrance and taste is like experiencing the Form Realm.

It is said that in the Formless Realm, all lust remaining in the Form Realm is extinguished. In the Formless Realm, the body comprising five sensory organs disappears, and only the mind organ (6th organ) and the mind information (6th object (boundary)) remain, causing the 6th consciousness. Only the three subrealms of mind organ, mind information, and 6th consciousness remain in the Formless Realm.

Three Subrealms in the Formless Realm

(Sense Organ)	~~Eye~~	~~Ear~~	~~Nose~~	~~Tongue~~	~~Body~~	Mind
	↓	↓	↓	↓	↓	↓
(Object)	~~Light (Color)~~	~~Noise~~	~~Scent~~	~~Flavor~~	~~Tactile Object~~	Mind Information
	↓	↓	↓	↓	↓	↓
(Consciousness)	~~Sight~~	~~Sound~~	~~Smell~~	~~Taste~~	~~Touch~~	Sixth Consciousness

It is said that the Formless Realm is a world that only saints who have attained complete enlightenment can enter.

Through dreams, we can experience the Hell World of the Desire Realm where the virtual body experiences pain and fear, and we can also experience the Form Realm without scent and taste. The Buddhist view of the universe which is divided into three Realms, the Desire Realm, the Form Realm, and the Formless Realm, and the Desire Realm consisting of 18 subrealms, the Form Realm of 14 subrealms, and the Formless Realm of 3 subrealms, is not a hypothesis to establish a religion, but a reasonable view of the universe classified from the viewpoint of consciousness.

Chapter 17
Thoughts and Awareness in Dreams

There is a story about a mathematician who found an answer to a math problem from a dream. Donald J. Newman, an American mathematician at MIT in the 1960s, was solving a tricky math problem, but at one point he got stuck. At the time, Newman was a member of a group of mathematicians formed at MIT, including John Nash, who later appeared as the main character in the movie <A Beautiful Mind>. Newman wrestled with the problem for about a week, and when he couldn't do anything about it, he had a dream. In the dream, he asked Nash who was with him at a restaurant in Cambridge about the problem, and found the answer by listening to Nash's explanation to do this and that. Of course, in reality, even Nash could not solve the problem. After Newman published a paper on the problem he had solved through dreams, he is said to have expressed his gratitude to Nash for contributing to the work even though the help came via a dream.

We think while we dream. Being afraid of a poisonous snake that attacks you in a dream is a proof that you are thinking. Everyone thinks and judges about the imagery in a dream, even if one does not have a logical mind to the extent of solving a math problem. In a dream, the functions of the five sense organs belonging to the body are temporarily suspended, but the mind organ continues to function and continues to think by accessing the mind information stored in the Alaya. As the mind organ works, the 7th consciousness, Manas, also works to turn the cycle of thoughts. During waking, the cycle of thought runs very quickly due to the large amount of information received through the five sense organs, but during sleep, the cycle of thoughts runs very slowly because there is no information received from the five sense organs and it depends only on the mind information contacted by the mind organ. Therefore, even if you think during dream, it will be often only a very fragmentary thought.

Although thoughts in dreams are fragmentary, they are common. And we all experience such thoughts in dreams. The important thing is to be aware of the dreams. While we are dreaming, we are unaware that it is a dream. They are mistaken as if the world they see in their dreams is the solid real world. However, there are times when we realize that it is a dream while we are dreaming. A dream in which we are aware that it is a dream is called a lucid dreaming.

The term 'lucid dreaming' was coined in a 1913 paper written by Frederik van Eeden, a Dutch psychiatrist. However, the concept of lucid dreaming was explained in different ways even in ancient times. In the 4th century B.C., when Aristotle made an apparent reference to lucid dreaming when he wrote of "something in consciousness which declares what then presents itself is but a dream." We should also note that Tibetan Buddhists have incorporated a form of lucid dreaming called dream yoga as part of their spiritual practices for more than 1,000 years.

The person who scientifically studied lucid dreaming was American neurophysiologist Steven LaBerge. According to his lucid dream survey in the 1980s, more than half of the respondents answered that they had a dream at least once in their lives in which they were vaguely aware that they were dreaming. One study found that 1 to 2% of subjects awakened during REM sleep were having lucid dreams. *The people who remember their dream well are found that they* were more likely to have lucid dreams.

Awareness in waking life is to look at the thought that arises and to look at the feeling or emotion that arises along with the thought, that is, the phenomena of the mind. It is to stop the discrimination or delusion which arises by turning the cycle of thoughts in the 7th consciousness (Manas), and become to be aware of the thoughts and mental phenomena In waking life, such awareness can be made volitionally. However, in dream, it is not easy to be aware of the dream volitionally. Therefore, in order to be aware of dreams, it is necessary to train to be aware of it in life.

According to one study, only 58 percent of people in the United States have experienced a lucid dream at least once in their lifetime. Twenty-one percent of them report having lucid dreams at least once a month. However, in a sample of people who had practiced Buddhist meditation or *transcendental meditation (*TM), the average number of lucid dream experiences rose to more than once a week.

Steven LaBerge also experienced lucid dreaming for the first time since childhood through a workshop organized by Tibetan monks. The Tibetan monks, who use lucid dreaming as part of their spiritual practices, taught them to consciously control the content of their dreams and regard reality as a dream. The Tibetan monks who organized the workshop stressed to the participants not to let go of their consciousness for 24 hours a day, and taught them to maintain self-reflective awareness even when dreaming.

In western science they infer that the brain has a relationship with lucid dreams as well as typical dreams. Alan Lechtschaffen, a dream researcher at the University of Chicago who studied brain imaging of lucid dreamers, says that the biggest feature of dreams is a lack of self-reflection, so we don't realize who we are while dreaming. He assumes that *the part of the brain that informs us about our state of consciousness is not working during a typical dream, but during a lucid dream it would be.* However, it is more likely that lucid dreams are also not caused by the brain, but the brain is activated by lucid dreams.

If our self-awareness of the mind organ is improved during real life and we become aware even in a dream, it is possible to act in a dream volitionally. We have an interpretation that if you dream of eating cooked rice, it is an omen of sickness. So, if possible, it is better not to eat cooked rice in a dream. If we realize that it is a dream and think that we should not eat cooked rice in the situation of eating in a dream, we can avoid the situation of eating. Thus, we can control the dream and prevent a possible sickness in reality by not eating cooked rice in the dream.

If we can think and be aware even in our dreams, we will not be dragged around by our dreams. We are attracted to our dreams because we are not aware of our dreams and mistake them for reality. This is also true in real life. Because we are not properly aware of reality, we are dragged around by desires and delusions. When we realize that our desires and delusions in reality are just dreams, we can be free from our obsession with the desires and delusions.

Chapter 18
Life is a Long Dream

There is a story that in an orthopedic hospital room, five or six patients, including those with disc problems and fractures, who could not move on their own, were lying down, and when a poisonous snake appeared in the room, all the patients who were lying down ran out of the room on their own. There is also a story that when a tiger was approaching a young child who had entered the zoo's tiger enclosure, the child's mother saved the child by bending the iron bars of the enclosure with her hands. There is a saying that even if you are captured by a tiger, you will survive as long as you wake up. They all show that we are capable of superhuman abilities depending on our mind or mental attitude.

We generally think that mind and spirit are more important than material things. Even if you are a materialist, it would be difficult to deny this idea. However, we believe that dreams seen with the mind organ while the body sleeps are fleeting and vain. It is thought that only what is perceived by the five sense organs attached to the body is solid. This is logically contradictory.

We think of dreams as ephemeral and futile, but in dreams they are very serious. Just like reality, we become obsessed with it, enjoy happiness, and suffer as much as reality in dreams. Only when we wake up do we realize that it was a fleeting and futile dream. It is the same in reality. Not knowing that this reality is a dream, we mistake it for something very solid and cling to it. In reality, we are obsessed with the five desires for the five external boundaries (objects) as well as the three desires (appetite, sleep, and lust) of the Desire Realm. Even if we make a lot of money, live affluently in a luxurious house, become successful, and enjoy power, when we look at it with the mind organ after the body is destroyed, it is a vain thing that cannot be taken away. Even dream researchers say that the real world we engage in when we are awake is a beautiful trick performed by extremely complex neural circuits. The external objects that have delighted the five sense organs for so long a life are nothing more than a dream of a spring day that is a bit longer than a dream of one night.

In the Diamond Sutra, the Buddha teaches "All composed things are like a dream, a phantom, a drop of dew, or a flash of lightning in the material world. That is how to meditate on them, that is how to observe them."

However, Buddhism does not advocate nihilism. Buddhism does not deny the existence of the external objects such as colors, sounds, flavors, tastes, and tactile objects, internal feeling such as pains, pleasures, thoughts, and emotions, and the external world of human beings. It's just that they are not the ultimate reality. It's just that is not a true self. It's just that you don't have to cling to the objects that don't have a true self, and it's not just that the existence of the external world is denied.

Humanity's ultimate goal is transcendence over the transitory. We perceive only the large-scale patterns into which more subtle phenomena organize themselves with our ordinary vision. Seeing only the patterns and not the underlying components, we are aware primarily of their differences. There is something important there that goes beyond the external world, so we should look for it. It can be the Buddha's nature that all sentient beings have, or it can be the four Wisdoms (Perfect Achievement Wisdom, Profound Contemplation Wisdom, Universal Equality Wisdom, and Great Mirror Wisdom) which are attained by transformation of the mental attributes of consciousness.

Once upon a time Zhuang Zhou dreamed he was a butterfly, a butterfly flitting about happily enjoying himself. He did not know whether he was Zhou, who had dreamed of being a butterfly, or a butterfly dreaming that he was Zhou. Then, he realized that when all things stand on the absolute stage where all things are united, Zhou, a human being, can be a butterfly, and the butterfly can also be Zhou. In a dream, he had obtained the Universal Equality Wisdom.

If we think that the five external objects contacted by the five sense organs are believed to be solidly real life, the sixth object (mind information) contacted by the sixth organ (mind organ) will also be solid real life. If so, the important messages that dreams give will not be considered fleeting. On the other hand, if the dream for the sixth organ to contact the sixth object is believed to be just a transitory dream, the real life for the five sense organs to contact the five external objects will also be just a transitory dream. If so, we can be freed from obsession with desire. Our self-views such as prejudice, preconception, delusions of discrimination, etc. stored in the Alaya will gradually disappear. Just as a large mirror reflects things as they really are, we will gain the Great Mirror Wisdom of seeing things as they really are.

PART 3 CONSCIOUSNESS AFTER DEATH

Chapter 19
The Unknown World of 'After-Death'

Buddhism explains that when a living thing dies, the physical body is scattered into four elements: earth, water, fire and wind. The solid components of the body are scattered into soil, the liquid components are scattered into water, the temperature of the body is scattered into heat, and the breath that comes and goes is scattered into wind. If the physical body is scattered like that, does anything continue to exist? Is everything ceased? While many people are committed to the belief that death brings the total cessation of personal existence, many others claim to be agnostic, quite honestly admitting that they don't know what happens at death and therefore have no views on the matter at all.

Regardless of whether we claim to be agnostic about death or not, the first question we will have concerning death is what existence will be like after death. Though we may suspect that there will exist something like a soul when a human body dies there is no scientific evidence to show it. There have been lots of attempts to prove it: some people have tried to take a picture of a soul, some have tried to record the voice of a soul, and some have tried to measure the weight of a soul. In spite of all these efforts, the life after death remains a mysterious domain to us.

In the scientific world, the brain is dead when the physical body dies, consciousness is dead when the brain is dead, and consciousness after death does not exist. They think that the death of the physical body is the final endpoint. Because the dominant western scientific view equates the mind with the brain, and the person with the mind, the objective of modern medicine has been to keep the brain alive, sometimes at the expense of other organ systems. If the brain is dead, western science seems not to consider it as worthy of additional research. Although experimental researches such as near-death studies have been carried out, the fundamental research on consciousness or mind seems not to have been carried out totally separated from the brain in western science.

Religion refutes science's position on the life of death. With science providing so little actual knowledge about the nature and origins of consciousness, so religion begs the question: what grounds do we have for the belief in eternal, mindless death when we die? As soothing as this notion may be, it is said to be little more than sheer conjecture at this point. Religion asserts that, moreover, science simply ignores the experiences of countless contemplatives throughout the world who have achieved deep states of meditative concentration and claim to have seen for themselves the existence of their own past lives. Religion asserts again that Buddhist contemplatives do not regard themselves in 'terrible muddle' with regard to consciousness, perhaps that's because they are part of a rigorous heritage that has taken the experiential investigation of consciousness very seriously for over two millennia, whereas modern science largely overlooked consciousness until the last decade of the twentieth century.

Each of the four major religions affirms that there is a subtle and death-surviving element—vital and psychical—in the physical body of flesh and blood. It may be a permanent entity or Self such as the Brahmanic *Atma*, the Islamic *Ruh*, and the Christian *Soul*, or it may be only a complex of activities (or *Skandha*), psychical and physical, with life as their function to the Buddhists. These *Skandha* do not constitute a simple Being or state of existence, but rather are a complex in continual change, and therefore, a series of physical and psychical momentary states successively generated the one from the other, a continuous transformation. Thus to none of these Faiths is death an absolute ending, but to all it is only the separation of the *Psyche* from the gross body.

All religions, including these four religions, admit the existence of soul or spirit. Though there are differences in detailed descriptions from religion to religion, they admit that something exists as psychical or physical (or consciousness) after death. On the other hand, all religions traditionally persuade people to lead a life of virtue due to fear of not only death, but also unknowns of the next life. When they assert the existence of soul or spirit after death it seems to be regarded not as a means for achieving the objective of religion by introducing the next life, but rather a result of insights and intuitions by the saints of each religion.

Chapter 20
Mechanism of After-Death Consciousness

I knew an L.A. woman who as a child had come home from school, and as she entered the door she saw her young cousin from Chicago standing in the corner waiting for her. Both were about eight at the time. The cousin didn't speak, and the girl ran to tell her mother that they had a visitor. When she entered the kitchen her mother was crying. The little girl asked why, and her mother said that there had been a sudden death in the family. It was the cousin from Chicago, who had died that morning. Did the girl see her cousin as a vision, a premonition, or merely as a coincidental act of imagination? As she tells the story, she saw her cousin 'for real.' Yet what do we mean by 'for real' except that something is convincing? This encounter with a departed relative can be judged as either hallucinatory or deeply spiritual depending not on the event itself but on who is looking at it.

This is from Deepak Chopra's "Life After Death". There are countless accounts of visions besides this LA girl's story. Since the soul is an immaterial being, it cannot be seen with the human eye. Nevertheless, we recognize something visually. This is seeing with the eye of mind, that is, with the mind eye in the mind organ.

Mind eye, mind year, mind nose, mind tongue and mind body are in the mind organ. In other words, it is to see the soul incarnated into a visual image with the mind eye in the mind organ. This means that the soul, an immaterial being, can be incarnated as a visual imagery.

Being able to see a visual imagery of the soul with the mind eye is like seeing things like the Eiffel Tower or the Statue of Liberty through visual imagery. The visual imagery to be seen with the mind eye is similar to hypnagogic imagery-hallucinatory visual images that occur as visual imagery before falling asleep or drifting off to sleep. In hypnagogic hallucinations, various visual imageries appear. Robert Stickgold, an assistant professor of psychiatry at Harvard, recalls his experience "After a day of hiking and rock climbing, as I drifted off to sleep, I immediately felt I was back on the mountain in one tricky passage where I had to cling to the rocks to pull myself up. I roused myself a couple of times, but each time I dozed off, the feeling of my hands on the rocks returned. Later in the night when I'd awake and try to get those same images back, I couldn't, but when I was first falling asleep they were unavoidable." If you are obsessed with billiards or golf when you are learning billiards or golf, it is like having a billiard ball or golf ball flickering in front of you even if you are lying down.

The soul can be manifested not only through visual images but also through imagery voices. We can hear certain voices from the soul. This is listening with the ear of the mind organ, that is, with the mind ear. It is like hearing a voice in a dream. The mind ear is also located in the mind organ (6th organ). It is to listen to the voice of the soul that has been manifested, with the mind ear within the mind organ. This means that the soul can be incarnated even through an imagery voice.

We usually refer to the visual image of the soul as a ghost, and the voice of the soul's image as the voice of a ghost. However, the visual imagery of the soul is not what one sees with the physical eye. Even the voices of the soul are not heard with the physical ear of the body. Therefore, they are called (visual) hallucination or auditory hallucination. In the field of medicine, the hallucinations are a kind of pathological symptom that occurs when the mind and body are not healthy. In a healthy state of mind and body, the five objects are properly perceived by the five sense organs, so we cannot see the visual images of the soul or hear the voices of the soul. Therefore, it can be said that ghosts do not exist for healthy people. However, like the child in LA who saw the relative child living in Chicago, one can see the visual imagery of the soul or hear the imagery voice of the soul in a state of purity and clarity of mind (mind organ). It is said that the practitioners who have entered the samadhi can see ghosts or hear the voices of ghosts in a state of awakening due to their high spiritual performance.

The presence or absence of consciousness is another important factor for the reality of the soul that is embodied in visual imagery or imagery voice. If the substance of the soul, which can be said to be a being in the afterlife, did not have consciousness like a stone on the roadside or a dry branch in the woods, the soul would not have been of interest to us. The reason why we view spirits and ghosts as objects of concern is because we think they have consciousness and so the ability to think.

Many religious Sages said "The consciousness does not die. It's only the body that dies." From the point of view of the Consciousness-Only Theory, the consciousness of the soul in the afterlife is similar to the dream consciousness during sleep. During sleep, the five sense organs are not functioning, so only the consciousness by the mind organ arises, and it becomes a dream. After death, since the body is destroyed, the five sense organs do not work, and only consciousness through the sixth organ occurs.

Mechanism of After-Death Consciousness

(Sense Organ)	~~Eye~~	~~Ear~~	~~Nose~~	~~Tongue~~	~~Body~~	Mind
(Object)	~~Light (Color)~~	~~Noise~~	~~Scent~~	~~Flavor~~	~~Tactile Object~~	Mind Information
(Consciousness)	~~Sight~~	~~Sound~~	~~Smell~~	~~Taste~~	~~Touch~~	Sixth Consciousness

The only difference between death and sleep is that sleep is a temporary inactivity of the five sense organs, followed by a restart when awakened from sleep. Thus, the five sense organs can return to a working state when awakened. But death is not like that. After the death of the body, the five sense organs can never be returned to working condition.

According to the Buddhist view of the universe, the soul that is not liberated remains in the realm of the Desire Realm among the three Realms even if the body is destroyed. However, in the Desire Realm, the virtual body (the body of consciousness) remains even if the physical body is dead, so the five sense organs (virtual organs) still exist, and the five sense consciousnesses arise through the five virtual organs.

Eighteen Subrealms in the Desire Realm

(Sense Organ)	Eye	Ear	Nose	Tongue	Body	Mind Organ
(Object)	Light (Color)	Noise	Scent	Flavor	Tactile Object	Mind Information
(Consciousness)	Sight	Sound	Smell	Taste	Touch	Sixth Consciousness

In the afterlife, only the mind organ comes into contact with the mind information (6th object) and raises consciousness, but a virtual body exists and will continue to live in the 18 subrealms as if a real body exists. So, just as the body and mind are terrified in a dream full of snakes, in the afterlife, we will feel either happiness or pain depending on the place either in heaven or in hell.

It is easy to think that all suffering disappears when the physical body dies, but just like in a dream, the conscious body (virtual) will share the pleasures or pains according to the karma it has done.

Chapter 21
Reincarnation

William George I was an excellent fisherman. He was an American Indian and believed in reincarnation like others of his tribe. He eagerly sought a rebirth as he was getting old, so he told his third son and daughter-in-law that if he gets a rebirth after death he wishes to be born as their son. He then showed them two spots on his body and told them that when they had a new son he would have the two spots on his body, indicating that the son is a reincarnation of him. One of the spots was on his left shoulder; the other was on his left elbow. He gave his third son a watch that was inherited from his mother, and told him to keep it safe for it would become evidence for his reincarnation later. Several weeks after that he went missing from the fishing boat he had worked. This was in August of 1949. Not long thereafter the third daughter-in-law became pregnant and had a baby on May 5, 1950. This was nine months since George I had gone missing. The daughter-in-law had a dream while she was in labor and was told by George I that he wished to see her son. She was surprisingly awakened from the dream and looked around because it seemed to her that George I was there. In the dream she saw George I just the same as the last image when he was alive.

The new baby was born with spots on his left shoulder and left elbow just as his grandfather, and due to this the baby was named George II. Growing up, it became certain that he was a reincarnation of his grandfather. He looked like his grandfather in his face, gait, character, etc. It seemed to them that he had a lot of knowledge on fishing and boats, and that he knew where the best bay for fishing was. One day he saw the watch in his mother's jewelry box and he told her "That is mine." His memory of the previous life faded out around ten.

The story above is one of twenty examples showing that a human being gets a rebirth as a human being after death which were recorded in the book *Eternal Freedom* of Korean Zen Master *Seong Chul*. Besides them, there are numerous examples about reincarnation of human beings after death. These have just not been proved scientifically.

According to a 1982 poll, one in four Americans believes in reincarnation. Considering the dominance of materialism and science in almost every aspect of everyday life, these findings are surprising. However, most people still have only the most shadowy idea about life after death, and no idea of what it might be like. Again and again, people tell me they cannot bring themselves to believe in something for which there is no evidence. But, there is no evidence that life after life does not exist either.

A lot of saints and sages who attained the highest enlightenment taught us that there are many previous lives as human beings, and reincarnation repeatedly happens. Such return to the earth plane takes place after release of the guilt of his sins in a state of 'Hell,' or the expiration of the term of enjoyment in 'Heaven' as he knows it, which his Karma has gained for him. However, most of the deceased take immediate rebirth on earth when they see visions of mating men and women. When they, at this final stage towards the awakening to earth-life, now know that they do not have a gross body of flesh and blood, they urgently desire to have one in order that they may again enjoy physical life on the earth world. Reincarnation is also recognized in psychology. The Freudian psychoanalyst will find herein a remarkable passage supporting his doctrine of the aversion of the son for the father.

In Buddhism, the soul of the afterlife is reincarnated and reborn in one World among the six Worlds of Human World, Animal World, Hell World, Hungry Ghost World, Warlike (Asura) World, and Heaven World. All of these are the world where sentient beings who have not extinguished their desires live, and they are in the Desire Realm. Among them, the Human World and Animal World are the physical world, a world in which they have physical bodies and operate their five sense organs. The Hell, Hungry Ghost, Asura, and Heaven are not the physical world, but the world of consciousness. In this type of consciousness world, the soul does not have a physical body, but a conscious body (virtual body).

When a soul is reincarnated, if the soul does not have any consciousness or any information for generating consciousness, that is, if it does not have any information about the previous lives, then the soul's reincarnation has no meaning. In order for the soul's reincarnation to have meaning, the soul must retain information about its previous lives. All of that information is stored in the Alaya of the soul. And that information is read by the immortal mind organ of the soul. In the end, the soul can be said to be a body of consciousness (continuum of consciousness) composed of mind organ, the subject of consciousness, and mind information, the object of consciousness, and the body of consciousness can be said to be the subject of reincarnation.

The book, *The Tibetan Book of The Dead*, which the founder of Tibetan Buddhism, Padma Sambhava, wrote, explains about the continuum of consciousness. According to the Tibetan theory of the book, the culminating process of death ends only upon the complete separation of the Bardo body from its earth-plane counterpart. The Bardo body means a continuum of consciousness at death. It is also called the Intermediary Being or the Middle Existence or frequently the Soul.

Bardo literally means 'between *Bar* and *do*;' i.e., 'between two states'—the state between death and rebirth—and, therefore, 'Intermediate' or 'Transitional' State. The different *bardos*, therefore, represent different states of consciousness of our life: the state of waking consciousness, the normal consciousness of a being born into our human world, known in Tibetan as the *skyes-nas bardo*; the state of dream consciousness (*rmi-lam bardo*); the state of *dhyana*, or trance consciousness, in profound meditation (*bsam-gtan bardo*); the state of the experiencing of death (*hchhi-kha bardo*); the state of experiencing of Reality (*chhos-nyid bardo*); the state of rebirth consciousness (*srid-pa bardo*).

In the *Hchhi-kha Bardo*, the deceased is, unless otherwise enlightened, more or less under the delusion that although he is deceased he still possesses a body like the body of flesh and blood. When he comes to realize that really he has no such body, he begins to develop an overwhelming desire to possess one; and, seeking for one, the *karmic* predilection for *sangsaric* existence naturally becoming all-determining, he enters into the *Srid-pa Bardo* of seeking Rebirth, and eventually, with his rebirth in this or some other world, the after-death state comes to an end.

Chapter 22
Why Don't We Remember Our Previous Lives?

"If we have lived before," I'm often asked, "why don't we remember it?" But why should the fact that we cannot remember our past lives mean that we have never lived before? After all, experiences of our childhood, or of yesterday, or even of what we were thinking an hour ago were vivid as they occurred, but the memory of them has almost totally eroded, as though they had never taken place. If we cannot remember what we were doing or thinking last Monday, how on earth do we imagine it would be easy, or normal, to remember what we were doing in a previous lifetime?

Many real examples of reincarnation have been reported, but because they cannot be scientifically proven, previous lives or reincarnations remain vague speculations. If everyone could remember their past lives, it would be easy to admit reincarnation. Unfortunately, most people cannot remember their past lives. Even if we sometimes remember our past lives, it is difficult to prove that the facts are correct.

Even if it is impossible to prove the facts about the previous life, humans have made great efforts to find the previous life. One of those methods is hypnosis. Hypnosis is one way to read the information about the previous life assuming that it is stored in the unconscious. Hypnosis is a technique that blocks the five senses and the 6th consciousness, and allows the mind organ to approach the unconscious (mind information in Alaya) and recognize the emerging consciousness.

Another possibility for reading information of the previous lives is in sleep dreams. During sleep, since the five objects are blocked, the mind organ can contact the information stored in the Alaya. At this time, if you come into contact with information about your previous lives, you can know your previous life. Carl Jung said that dreams are a product of the collective unconscious, seeing content that he had never experienced before appearing in dreams. The collective unconscious refers to the unconscious depth that reflects the inherited experiential record of the human species. From a perspective of the Consciousnees-Only Theory, the collective unconscious can be said to be information regarding previous lives which are stored in the Alaya.

It is said that one can know one's previous lives through meditation. As a result of intensive practice in long, meditative retreats, some experience of deeper clarity occurs, and at that moment people recall their past life. Some of them have been able to recall twenty or thirty lifetimes, some even during the Buddha's time. It is said that as the transparency of consciousness is enhanced through meditation practice, the memory becomes very clear. That means the power of memory is increasing, so automatically the memory of the previous lives would also increase.

Reincarnating in a new body and reading mind information about the previous life is like waking up and remembering yesterday's information. Even if you sleep, the information of yesterday before sleeping does not disappear. When you wake up, the memories of the past are retained again. There is sleep as a gap between yesterday and today, but it is not difficult to recall the consciousness of yesterday. But if you are born again after death, why do you not remember the information of your previous life? There is death as a gap between the previous life and the present life, so it is much more difficult to remember the previous life. Why?

There is a difference in the continuity of language and letters between the awakened state and the reincarnated state. Sleep does not affect the continuity of language and writing, but the death of the body cuts off that continuity. I don't forget what I said or wrote just because I slept. However, reincarnation from death makes them unable to speak and unable to write. Upon awakening, the mind organ reads yesterday's information stored in Alaya and expresses and communicates it using words or letters. If reincarnated, the mind organ can also read the information of his previous life stored in Alaya. But unfortunately, there is no way to express it.

The mind organ and the mind information stored in Alaya exist always there, transcending time and space. But in the beginning, there were no words. It's not like there were letters in the beginning. Language or text is just a tool created by humans for communication. Even animals have their own too, although it is extremely limited. Language is a habitual product of all animals, including humans. Because I was born in Korea, I was able to learn the Korean language habitually. It takes a lot of time to learn language and texts.

If human beings were able to speak as soon as they were born, they would be able to remember and express the information about their past lives stored in their Alaya consciousness as if they had just woken up from sleep. But it cannot be, because speech is a product of habit. Humans are born and learn to speak as they grow up. By the time he is two or three years old, he can pick up easy words and start simple communication. It is said that children sometimes talk about their previous lives at the point when they learn to speak and start expressing their opinions. At that point, all of a sudden, they say things like, "I am such and such a person who lived at such and such a place before."

Children of two or three or four who are just starting to learn to speak are illiterate and do not know the language well, so much information from the present life has not yet been entered into their Alaya. The information of the previous life is gathered on the surface of their Alaya, and such information easily comes into contact with the mind organ. If they say something out of the blue when you have never studied or experienced anything as a child, it is highly likely that it is about the previous life. However, it is not common to say even a few words like that. If we look at the growth process of a child, we can understand why.

It shouldn't be surprising that children of ages one to three who begin to learn some words sometimes talk about things concerning their previous lives. A lot of information on the previous life may remain at the surface of Alaya and be easy to recall, and a lot of new information has not yet been input through the five organs. They, of course, begin to learn a spoken language and written letters from birth and this begins to input new information in their Alaya. In fact, the previous life is not an important concern for them; their major concern is about the five sense objects. The imminent things for them at the 'now' moment are to fill their hungry stomach and to avoid the hot or cold. As they grow and learn a spoken language and written letters, a lot of new information on the sense objects are input through the corresponding five organs and stored in Alaya. The information on the previous life is covered with the new information and stored more deeply in Alaya, and is therefore getting more difficult to recall.

However, it is a very natural providence that reincarnation after death cuts off the continuity of language and letters. If reincarnation after death did not cut off the continuity of language and letters, and if it were possible to remember and express all previous lives as if waking up from sleep, the human world would be very confused.

According to the Consciousness-Only Theory, the sixth organ (mind organ) is the only means or program which can read the past-life information, but we have never operated this program, never tried to access it during our lifetime. We contact the five objects and operate the five organs so as to stimulate the thinking cycle from birth—our life is heavily oriented toward seeking the five objects in order to satisfy the five organs. Although the sixth organ has the ability to read mind information including previous lives, the sixth is not trained to do it, but is trained by our intellect to read the information which is generated by the five organs. We are not trained to stop the random thinking process so as to read the information of previous lives which is stored in Alaya. Just as we cannot read without learning letters and we cannot speak without learning spoken words, it is impossible to read the information of Alaya without learning how to do it.

Chapter 23
The Driving Force for Reincarnation – Karma

In Buddhism, the soul of the afterlife is reincarnated and reborn in one World among the six Worlds of Human World, Animal World, Hell World, Hungry Ghost World, Warlike (Asura) World, and Heaven World. Among them, the Human World and Animal World are the physical world, a world in which they have physical bodies and operate their five sense organs. The reincarnation of the soul after death means being reborn in the Human World or the Animal World. However, it is said that human beings, who are the best beings in the physical world, do not become animals at once, no matter how heinous their sins. It is said that there is no sudden jump from animal to human or from human to animal. Then, human beings must be reborn as human beings. Even if someone commits one of five cardinal sins and goes to hell, when his life there ends, he must be reborn as a human being.

According to [The Tibetan Book of The Dead], the soul of a dead person passes through Bardo, the world of dreams, and enters the womb of a human with flesh and bones. The soul begins its physical growth in the womb of its own choosing and is born as a human being. Intercourse with parents is a volitional act, but it is up to the soul to choose the parents.

If it is true for the continuum of consciousness to be reborn, what will be the nature of rebirth? Is rebirth random? Why is someone born in wealth, while someone else is born in poverty? If there is coherence to rebirth, what is the nature of that coherence? The Buddha's claim was that, from the perspective of an awakened awareness, there is coherence—certain types of actions give rise to certain types of consequences. The coherence is called karma.

'Karma' is the Sanskrit word for 'action' or 'deed', but the actual meaning is more complicated than this. In anthropological terminology, 'karma' is a thick, theory-laden term. Karma refers to the nature of actions and how their long-term consequences play out over time.

Karma is also said as a result of an action, and that karma is information with power or energy derived from the action. That information is stored intact in the Alaya. Karma is the fundamental morality of Buddhism, which has the same system as the precepts, and is defined as the three karmas of body, mouth and mind. The karma of being made by the body is the karma of body ('body karma'), the karma of being made by the mouth is the karma of mouth ('mouth karma'), and the karma of being made by the mind is the karma of mind ('mind karma'). Right actions, right words, and right thinking can make the three good karmas.

There are three types of bad karmas in the body karma: killing, stealing, and adultery, four types of bad karmas in the mouth karma: lying, false speech, alienating remarks, and bad mouth, and three types of mind karmas: covetousness (greed), sincerity (anger), and foolishness (delusion). If you do them rightly, you will perform the Ten Good Karmas, and if you do contrary to them, you will perform the Ten Bad Karmas. Depending on whether you do good or bad karma, karma creates energy accordingly.

In the Consciousness-Only Theory, karma is the energy obtained from actions and is called habit energy, which means the power or energy accumulated by habits or actions, and the energy of karma is said to be the driving force for reincarnation.

In other words, the bad karma is resentment (hostility). The greater the resentment, the greater the power of karma. The greatest resentment of all is that one's own life is killed. The most important precept not only in Buddhism but also in all religions is the precept of non-killing. It means not killing another life as well as themselves. This is because the strongest bad karma is created when someone is killed. Taking one's own life is also planting a powerful karma of resentment in one's soul.

Whoever kills another life will be rewarded by that powerful karma of the dead. The strong karmic spirit created when killed seeks an opportunity to seek revenge by seeking out the soul of the perpetrator. The soul of the victim looking for the soul of the perpetrator is not even a task for the soul that travels beyond time and space. It could be a series of retaliations. In order to break this vicious cycle, we must release the resentment of the karma. Requesting repentance from those who have sinned and granting forgiveness to those who are unfair is to break the vicious circle by releasing the resentment of karma.

The cycle of reincarnation never runs down. The cycle of existence from rebirth to rebirth is like being a ball in a perpetual motion pinball machine. The cycle runs of its own momentum as long as it is fueled by the same habitual patterns. Reincarnation proceeds by the habitual energy contained in karma. The Buddhist hypothesis is that the cycle of reincarnation stops only when we take radical measures and break through the habitual patterns of delusion.

Buddhist teachings are able to nullify the negative karmic seeds that are etched into the stream of consciousness. Actions cannot be undone, but it is possible to purify the streams of the consciousness so that the effects of the karmic seeds are negated. In order to neutralize karma, which is the driving force of reincarnation, the energy of resentment must be extinguished. Ultimately, we must reach the state of the ultimate Wisdom, that is, the state of enlightenment.

Buddhism teaches that human beings can reach the ultimate Wisdom only through the individual practice. It depends on the individual's consciousness whether he will die with the belief that happiness by the five objects in the present life is the highest because he believes nothing exists after death or doesn't know about the world, whether he will die storing in Alaya the belief that, when he dies, the Absolute God will save his after-death life, or whether he will try to empty Alaya so as to reach the Wisdom through the awareness that there exists merely Consciousness regardless of life and death, and that all dharmas are manifested by the Consciousness. We will meet the right one depending on the individual's karma.

PART 4 CONSCIOUSNESS-ONLY THEORY AND DIAMOND SUTRA

Chapter 24
The Diamond Sutra - "Practical Principles on Mind"

The Diamond Sutra is the most fundamental sutra among eighty thousand sutras in Korean and Chinese Buddhism. The Diamond Sutra is composed of only 5,149 Chinese letters in a total 32 Chapters. If we recite it aloud, it will take about 30 minutes.

The Diamond Sutra is a sutra that Shakyamuni Buddha preached in dialogue with the Venerable Subhuti, one of the Buddha's 12 disciples, at a gathering of 1,250 Buddhist monks. The Buddha answers questions from the Venerable Subhuti, and the Buddha himself answers after asking the Venerable Subhuti questions. When we recite the Sutra, we can feel like we are vividly listening to the Buddha's sermon.

However, in the Sutra, which is important enough

to be regarded as the most important scripture in Korea and China, there is no content that worships the Buddha or praises the Buddha's power. It does not teach us about the Five Precepts, the Four Noble Truths, or the Noble Eightfold Paths. There is no content to keep the precepts such as non-killing or show mercy.

The Sutra speaks only of the mind. The first question of the Venerable Subhuti in the Sutra is how to put forth one's mind in order to attain the supreme perfect universal enlightenment (the mind of a state where all wisdom has been awakened to the highest level of wisdom). In order to do so, the Buddha says that one must abandon one's self-view (ego) (Chapter 3 of the Sutra). This is the first preach of the Buddha in the Sutra.

The self-view is again classified into four fundamental defilements (vexing passions): self-delusion, self-belief, self-conceit, and self-love. Self-delusion means lack of understanding. It means ignorance of the true nature of the Atman (the 'inner self' or 'higher self') or individual divine essence, and delusion as to the principle that there is no Atman (egolessness). Self-belief means adhering to the view that Atman exists, erroneously imagining certain dharmas (transitory conditions which cause creation) to be the self when they are not so. Self-conceit means pride; basing itself on the belief in an Atman, it causes the mind to feel superior and lofty. Self-love means a greedy desire for the self; because of its belief in the Atman it develops deep attachments to it. The four vexing passions are from the wrong view that we believe in 'individual ego' and attach to it. In other words, the self-view is explained as the idea that a self exists. Further, the Buddha teaches that one must abandon one's person-view, living being-view, and life span-view. The person-view is an idea that a person exists, the living bing-view is an idea that a living being exists, and the life span-view is an idea that a life span-view exists. The Buddha repeats fifteen times in the Diamond Sutra that one must abandon the four views in order to be an authentic bodhisattva.

The second preach of the Buddha in the Sutra is that a bodhisattva should practice generosity without relying on any object, that is, any form (color), sound, smell, taste, tactile object, or dharma (Chapter 4 of the Sutra). Further, the Buddha says that, if a bodhisattva practice generosity without relying on the objects, the happiness that results cannot be conceived of or measured. It is like the Bible says, don't let your left hand know what your right hand is doing.

As a third preach, the Buddha said to Subhuti, "In a place where there is something that can be distinguished by forms (objects), in that place there is deception. If you can see the formless nature of forms, then you can see the Tathagata (reality)" (Chapter 5 of the Sutra). This means that since the concepts, ideas, images, or mental phenomena of the objects could deceive you, do not be deceived by them. We may be deceived by the drunken appearance of a person and we cannot see the true nature of him or her. If you are not deceived, you can see the reality or true nature of the objects, and further, the Tathagata, the Buddha nature.

Of the 32 Chapters of the Diamond Sutra, excluding the first two Chapters for the preparation of the sermon, the remaining 30 Chapters are the contents of the Dharma sermon concerning mind in this way. In Chapter 10 of the Sutra, the Buddha teaches about how to give rise to a pure and clear mind: that is "In order to give rise to a pure and clear mind, all the bodhisattvas should not rely on forms (colors), sounds, smells, tastes, tactile objects, or dharmas (objects of mind: mind information). They should give rise to the mind without relying on any of the objects." This teaching is the heart of the Diamond Sutra. It is said that many Buddhists have attained enlightenment from the teachings of Chapter 10. The Sutra explains about how to give rise to a pure and clear mind by citing the six objects: forms (colors), sounds, smells, tastes, tactile objects, or dharmas. Any Sutra in other religions does not explain about the six objects. Buddhism is probably the only religion that preaches on the six objects (boundaries) in the Sutra. As such, the Diamond Sutra contains the core of the Consciousness-Only Philosophy.

And, there are two things that are repeated and emphasized throughout the Sutra. One of them is not to be deceived by name and color (form or object), but to look at the reality or the true nature. In the Sutra the Buddha said that He had not taught about self-view, even though he had. Why? Because the self-view is not self-view, but the name of it. Likewise, the mind is not mind, but the name of it. Such teachings repeat thirty times in the Sutra. The reason for such repeating is not to attach to the concepts, ideas, images, or mental phenomena of the objects, but to see the reality or true nature of them. Thus, the Buddha said "Someone who looks for me in form or seeks me in sound is on a mistaken path and cannot see the Tathagata (Chapter 26 of the Sutra)."

The second emphasis is on the immeasurable blessings of the Diamond Sutra. In the Sutra, the Buddha teaches "Someone who accepts the Buddha's teachings and puts them into practice, even if only a gatha (an abridged verse of the Buddha's teaching) of four lines, and explains them to someone else brings more happiness than someone who fills the 3,000 chiliocosms [worlds] with the seven precious treasures as an act of generosity (Chapters 8, 11, 13 and 24 of the Sutra)." The Sutra repeats such teaching nine times. If you do not understand the importance of the Alaya consciousness, you will regard this teaching as an exaggerated metaphor; but, if you understand the importance of the Alaya consciousness as the basis of the Manas consciousness, you will understand that this teaching is not an exaggeration. The seven precious treasures amounting to the number of sands in the Ganges does not contribute any help to the production of a pure mind. Instead, they will contribute to produce a desire or a craving. The information that should be stored in the Alaya in order to produce a pure mind is the Buddha's teachings such as the gathas instead of the precious treasures. The teachings stored in the Alaya may lead to wisdom and ultimately enlightenment.

In conclusion, the Buddha teaches "All composed things are like a dream, a phantom, a drop of dew, or a flash of lightning. That is how to meditate on them, that is how to observe them (Chapter 32 of the Sutra)." This is not to cling to the six objects, colors (forms), sounds, smells, tastes, tactile objects and objects of mind, but to see the ultimate reality through the Mind.

Chapter 25
Summary of the Consciousness-Only Theory

The Mere-Consciousness Doctrine was originated by the Buddha, and theoretically systemized by Maitreya (A.D 270-350). Following thereafter, Asanga (A.D 300-389) and his brother, Vasubandhu (A.D 320-400) completed the philosophy.

Asanga, who was born in Gandhara, Northern India, began as a Hinayana Buddhist but later became a Mahayanan. He wrote two major books. One is Samdhinirmocana Sutra which annotated Madhyamaka Sutra of Nagarjuna, the other is Mahynasamgraha in which the Mere-Consciousness doctrine is organized based on the Mahayana Abhidharma Sutra.

Vasubandhu, like his elder brother, Asanga, began as a Hinayana Buddhist but also later became a Mahayanan. He made remarkable achievement on the Mere-Consciousness philosophy and wrote two books: Vijnaptimatratasiddhi-trimsika (Trimsika: Thirthy Stanzas on Mere-Consciousness) and *Wei-shih Erh Shih Lun* (Vimsatika: Twenty Treatises on Mere-Consciouness). The Thirty Stanzas are very brief, like a poem with no annotation. Therefore, a lot of sastra-masters wrote commentaries on the Thirty Stanzas so as to further develop the Mere-Consciousness philosophy. The Thirty Stanzas later became the basis of Hsuan Tsang's masterpiece, *Ch'eng Wei-shih-Lun.*

The Mere-Consciousness philosophy was spread into China to found the Fa-hsiang (Dharmalaksana: Vijinaptimatrata) school. The Fa-hsiang school originated from Hsuan Tsang (A.D 602-664) who studied the Mere-Consciousness philosophy in India. He wrote *Ch'eng Wei-shih-Lun* (Treatise on the Doctrine of Mere-Consciousness) which annotated the Thirty Stanzas and became the cornerstone of the Fa-hsiang school. In fact it was Hsuan Tsang's most eminent disciple, Kuei Chi, who wrote a Commentay on *Ch'eng Wei-shih-Lun* (a work of outstanding excellence) and became the founder of the Fa-hsiang school. As the Fa-hsiang school emphasized the Middle Way of No-existence and No-emptiness, it was called a Middle Way school. The philosophy of Fa-hsiang adopted many doctrines of the Mere-Consciousness philosophy of India, including among them the eight consciousnesses doctrine including Alaya consciousness (Alayavijnana).

The Thirty Stanzas by Vasubandhu is a foundation of the Mere-Consciousness philosophy. The framework of the Mere-Consciousness was made by Maitreya and Asanga, and the systematic completion was achieved in the Thirty Stanzas by Vasubandhu. The translation of the Thirty Stanzas into Chinese by Hsuan Tsang is composed of only thirty songs like poems. Each song has only twenty Chinese letters in four phrases. The Thirty Stanzas consists of only 600 Chinese letters.

The Thirty Stanzas contain the essence about consciousness. Realizing that the Thirty Stanzas was replete with intricate and profound meanings, Vasubandhu had intended to write his own commentary on it but he died before doing so. Subsequently, the task of expounding the philosophy underlying the Thirty Stanzas fell to ten sastra-masters, each of whom composed a commentary on them. These ten sastra-masters are Bandhusri, Cittrabhanu, Gunamati, Sthiramati, Nanda, Shuddhacandra, Dharmapala, Jnamitra, Jinapura and Jnanacandra. Hsuan Tsang authored *Ch'eng Wei-shih-Lun* based on the Thirty Stanzas, a creative and elaborate exposition of the Thirty Stanzas and a synthesis of the ten commentaries.

Ch'eng Wei-shih-Lun represents the power of Hsuan Tsang and his disciple Kuei Chi's literary and spiritual genius. This work is enormous compared with the Thirty Stanzas, as it consists of ten Chinese volumes. As the book was synthesized with the ten commentaries, various different views were also introduced. According to the book there are many agreeable aspects, but there are also many different views on the consciousness doctrines. For example, according to Mere-Consciousness, each sentient being has a fundamental consciousness (Alayvijnana: Storchouse Consciousness), which evolves in a homogeneous and continuous series and carries within it the 'seeds' (Bijas) of all dharmas. In regard to the origin of Bijas, one theory asserts that they are all inborn and natural; i.e., innately existing in Alaya consciousness, and none of them come into being as a result of causality. However, another theory explains that Bijas are all born as a result of causation. A third theory is that there are actually two kinds of Bijas. Some Bijas are natural or inborn, other Bijas are those whose existence has had a beginning and come into being as a result of being caused by actual dharmas. As shown in the example above, different views in many aspects remain unchanged with not much progress for more than 1,000 years.

The Thirty Stanzas consists of three parts, a first part from the first stanza to the nineteenth, a second from the twentieth to the twenty-fifth, and a third from the twenty-sixth to the thirtieth. The first part explains the principles and mechanism of eight consciousnesses, the second part explains the natures of consciousness, and the third part explains the holy path of attainment in which five stages for obtaining Buddhahood through the Mere-Consciousness doctrine are explained.

According to the Consciousness-Only Theory there are eight consciousnesses, which are the first six consciousnesses by the six organs, Manas consciousness as the seventh, and Alaya consciousness as the eighth. The Theory has three important characteristics.

The first important characteristic of the Consciousness-Only Doctrine is in the eighth consciousness, Alaya, which is a storehouse for storage of all consciousnesses. All the six consciousnesses and the seventh, including mental activities, are stored in Alaya without exception. Strictly speaking, Alaya is not a kind of consciousness. Just as sound or smell is not a truly a kind of consciousness, so neither is Alaya. Alaya is deemed as a storehouse of all consciousnesses which we perceived, thought and felt. Alaya is like a database in which all data are stored. Alaya contains all the seven consciousnesses. It does not matter whether the consciousness has been acknowledged or not. Further, Alaya contains not only all consciousnesses of the present life, but also of all the previous lives. Alaya is a formative element in birth and rebirth. Alaya in Buddhism corresponds to the unconscious or subconscious in psychology or psychoanalysis.

The second important characteristic of the Consciousness-Only Theory is in the seventh consciousness, Manas. It has the nature and character of cogitation or intellection, and is called 'cogitation consciousness.' According to *Ch'eng Wei-shih-Lun,* Manas consciousness manifests itself with Alayavijnana as its basis and support, and takes Alayavijnana as its object. The Consciousness-Only Theory separates cogitation consciousness from the six sense consciousnesses by introducing Manas. It has not been introduced either in psychology or psychoanalysis, though thinking or thought consciousness is not denied. Western science in particular believes that the process of thinking is carried out in the brain, and they cannot imagine the process of cogitation without the brain. In the Consciousness-Only Theory, however, Manas is not explained as correlating with either the brain or any other physical organ. The seventh consciousness as Manas can be explained a continuation process of the sixth consciousness.

The third important characteristic of the Consciousness-Only Doctrine is in the sixth consciousness, Manovijnana. There is no doubt about the first five consciousnesses, but the sixth is not straight forward. The first five consciousness are called 'sense consciousnesses,' while the sixth 'sense-centre consciousness.' The sixth consciousness is generated by the sixth organ which is explained as 'organ of Mind' or 'root of Mind.' It is clear that the sixth organ is not the brain. It must be a non-physical and immaterial organ, but it is capable of reading mind information, resulting in generating a sixth consciousness, Manovijnana.

The second part of The Thirty Stanzas, from the twentieth to the twenty-fifth, explains about the natures of consciousness. They are nature of mere-imagination, nature of dependence on others, and ultimate reality. The nature of mere-imagination of consciousness means that the reality of things is assumed by imagination. This is an illusion, for things are imagined to really exist where in fact there are none. It is like seeing a mirage which vanishes as one approaches it. Imagined objects have, therefore, no objective reality. However, the first five and the eighth consciousnesses do not have the nature of mere-imagination. Only the sixth and the seventh are possessed of the faculty of imagination. The nature of dependence on others means that all discriminations by consciousness are produced by causes and conditions. There is nothing self-existing in the world, everything depends for its existence on something else, things are universally mutually conditioned, endlessly related one to another. The ultimate reality, as the third nature, means the genuine nature of consciousness thus revealed by the Emptiness or Voidness (*sunyata*) of Atman and dharma. The ultimate reality is the complete and perfect 'real nature' of all dharmas.

Buddhism describes the transformation of the Eight Consciousnesses into the Four Wisdoms. The Consciousness-Only Theory explains that four transcendental wisdoms are attained by transformation of the mental attributes of consciousness. The Four Wisdoms are the Perfect Achievement Wisdom, the Profound Contemplation Wisdom, the Universal Equality Wisdom, and the Great Mirror Wisdom. The Perfect Achievement Wisdom is attained by virtue of the transformation of the five sense consciousnesses, the Profound Contemplation Wisdom by the transformation of the sixth, the Universal Equality Wisdom by the transformation of the seventh, and the Great Mirror Wisdom by the transformation of the eighth. The Perfect Achievement Wisdom must be attained through living in the material world which obeys the laws of nature; i.e., water always flows to a lower level, the law of gravity applies to all objects, an onion will not produce a rose, and as one sows so shall he reap, etc. The Profound Contemplation Wisdom is attained by the transformation of the sixth consciousness. With this Wisdom the sixth organ (Mind) perceives the sixth objects (mind information) with profound clarity and without hindrance. This is the spiritual world where the mind organ experiences wonderful observations. If the Profound Contemplation Wisdom is attained the mind organ can see unseeable objects, hear soundless sounds, smell scentless scents, taste food without flavor, and be free from space and time. The Universal Equality Wisdom is attained by the transformation of the seventh consciousness. The mind associated with this Wisdom sees the identity of all dharmas, and the complete equality between its own self and other sentient beings. The Great Mirror Wisdom is attained by the transformation of the eighth consciousness. The mind associated with this Wisdom is entirely dissociated from all mental discriminations. The Great Mirror is free from errors in its perception of all objects. Like a big mirror reflects all objects as they are, this Wisdom reflects the absolute reality of all things as they are.

BIBLIOGRAPHY

Merriam-Webster's Collegiate Dictionary, Eleventh Edition. (2003). (F. C. Mish Ed. 11th ed.). Springfield, MA: Merriam Webster, Inc.

Amen, D. G. (1998). *Change your brain, change your life : the breakthrough program for conquering anxiety, depression, obsessiveness, anger, and impulsiveness* (1st ed.). New York: Times Books.

Atkins, P. W. (2003). *Galileo's Finger: the Ten Great Ideas of Science.* Oxford; New York: Oxford University Press.

Brockman, J., & OverDrive Inc. (2013). *Thinking the new science of decision-making, problem-solving, and prediction* (pp. 1 online resource). Retrieved from http://princeton.lib.overdrive.com/ContentDetails.htm?ID=8BE117A2-7BB6-4097-97B2-A5364EFD181A

Bstan 'dzin rgya, m., Varela, F. J., & Engel, J. (1997). *Sleeping, dreaming, and dying : an exploration of consciousness with the Dalai Lama ; foreword by H.H. the Fourteenth Dalai Lama ; narrated and edited by Francisco J. Varela ; with contributions by Jerome Engel, Jr. ... [et al.] ; translations by B. Alan Wallace and Thupten Jinpa.* Boston: Wisdom Publications.

Capra, F. (2010). *The tao of physics : an exploration of the parallels between modern physics and Eastern mysticism* (5th ed.). Boston: Shambhala.

Choi, D. (2011). *Mechanism of consciousness during life, dream and after-death*. Bloomington, IN: AuthorHouse.

Chopra, D. (2006). *Life after death : the burden of proof* (1st ed.). New York: Harmony Books.

Conze, E. (2001). *Buddhist wisdom : containing the Diamond Sutra and the Heart Sutra* (1st ed.). New York: Vintage Books.

Cook, F. H., Xuanzang, Vasubandhu, Xuanzang, Vasubandhu, & Numata Center for Buddhist Translation and Research. (1999). *Three texts on Consciousness Only : Demonstration of Consciousness Only*. Berkeley, Calif.: Numata Center for Buddhist Translation and Research.

Doidge, N. (2007). *The brain that changes itself : stories of personal triumph from the frontiers of brain science*. New York: Viking.

Dossey, L. (2013). *One Mind: How Our Individual Mind is Part of a Greater Consciousness and Why It Matters* (1st edition. ed.) Hay House, Inc.

Evans-Wentz, W. Y., Karma glin, p., & Zla ba bsam, g. (1960). *The Tibetan book of the dead; or, The after-death experiences on the Bardo plane, according to Lāma Kazi*

Dawa-Samdup's English rendering (3d ed.). New York,: Oxford University Press.

Gelernter, D. (2014, January 2014). *The Closing of the Scientific Mind*. Commentary Magazine.

Goldstein, J. (1976). *The experience of insight : a natural unfolding*. Santa Cruz: Unity Press.

Goswami, A. (2007). *Mind Before Matter: Visions of a New Science of Consciousness* (J. E. M. a. P. D. Trish Pfeiffer Ed.). New Alresford, Hampshire, UK: IFF Books.

Goswami, A., Reed, R. E., & Goswami, M. (1993). *The self-aware universe: how consciousness creates the material world*. New York: Putnam's Sons.

Grimes, R. (2010). *The Fun of Dying: Find Out What Really Happens Next!* (1st ed.): Greater Reality Publications.

Hanh, T. N., Laity, A., & Nguyen, A. H. (2010). *The diamond that cuts through illusion commentaries on the Prajñaparamita Diamond Sutra* (pp. 1 online resource (150 p.)). Retrieved from http://libproxy.lib.unc.edu/login?url=http://site.ebrary.com/lib/uncch/Doc?id=10469185

Hart, W. (1987). *The art of living : Vipassana meditation as taught by S.N. Goenka* (1st ed.). San Francisco: Harper & Row.

Ickes, W. J. (2003). *Everyday mind reading : understanding what other people think and feel.* Amherst, N.Y.: Prometheus Books.

Jotika, U. (2008). *Geography of Mind* (E. Park, Trans.). Seoul, S. Korea: Yonbangjuk.

Jung, C. G. (1966). *Two essays on analytical psychology* (2d ed.). New York: Pantheon.

Koch, C. (2004). *The Quest for consciousness : a neurobiological approach.* Englewood, CO: Roberts and Company Publishers.

Kyabgon, T. (2001). *The essence of Buddhism : an introduction to its philosophy and practice.* Boston: Shambhala.

LaBerge, S. (2009). *Lucid dreaming : a concise guide to awakening in your dreams and in your life.* Boulder, Colo.: Sounds True.

Mahesh, Y. (2001). *Science of being and art of living : transcendental meditation* (Newly rev. & updated. ed.). New York, N.Y.: Plume.

Nagasawa, Y. (2008). *God and phenomenal consciousness: a novel approach to knowledge arguments.* Cambridge; New York: Cambridge University Press.

Nagel, T. (2012). *Mind and Cosmos: Why the Materialist Neo-Darwinian Conception of Nature Is Almost Certainly False.* New York: Oxford University Press.

Nhat, H. n., Laity, A., & Nguyen, A. H. (2010). *The diamond that cuts through illusion : commentaries on the Prajñaparamita Diamond Sutra* (Rev. ed.). Berkeley, Calif.: Parallax Press.

Nisargadatta. (1973). *I am that*. Bombay: Chetana.

Nisbett, R. E. (2003). *The geography of thought : how Asians and westerners think differently-- and why*. New York: Free Press.

Pearce, J. C. (1992). *Evolution's end: claiming the potential of our intelligence* (1st ed.). San Francisco: HarperSanFrancisco.

Pinker, S. (1997, 2009). *How the mind works* (Norton pbk. ed.). New York: Norton.

Poppe, N. (1971). *The Diamond Sutra; three Mongolian versions of the Vajracchedika Prajñāpāramita*. Wiesbaden,: Harrassowitz.

Radin, D. I. (2013). *Supernormal: science, yoga, and the path to extraordinary psychic abilities* (First edition. ed.) New York, Random House, Inc, Deepak Chopra Books

Radin, D. I. (1997). *The conscious universe: the scientific truth of psychic phenomena* (1st. ed.).NewYork,N.Y.:HarperEdge.

Rock, A. (2004). *The mind at night : the new science of how and why we dream* (1st ed.). New York: Basic Books.

Schrœdinger, E., & Schrœdinger, E. (2012). *What is life? : the physical aspect of the living cell ; with, Mind and matter ; & Autobiographical sketches* (Canto ed.). Cambridge ; New York: Cambridge University Press.

Sharma, R. S. (1998). *The monk who sold his Ferrari : a fable about fulfilling your dreams and reaching your destiny* (1st ed.). San Francisco: HarperSanFrancisco.

Sheldrake, R. (2012). *Science set free: 10 paths to new discovery*. New York: Deepak Chopra Books.

Sogyal, R., Gaffney, P. D., & Harvey, A. (2002). *The Tibetan book of living and dying* (10th anniversary ed.). London: Rider.

Stanford University., & Center for the Study of Language and Information (U.S.). (1997 (with quarterly updates)). *Stanford encyclopedia of philosophy* Retrieved from http://openurl.cdlib.org/?sid=UCB:CAT&genre=article&issn=1095-5054

Tenzin, P. (2002). *Reflections on a mountain lake : teachings on practical Buddhism*. Ithaca, N.Y.: Snow Lion Publications.

Tucker, J. B. (2013). *Return to life: extraordinary cases of children who remember past lives* (First Edition. ed.). New York: St. Martin's Griffin.

Varela, F. J., Bstan 'dzin rgya, m., & Engel, J. (1997). *Sleeping, dreaming, and dying : an exploration of consciousness with the Dalai Lama ; foreword by H.H. the Fourteenth Dalai Lama ; narrated and edited by Francisco J. Varela ; with contributions by Jerome Engel, Jr. ... [et al.] ; translations by B. Alan Wallace and Thupten Jinpa.* Boston: Wisdom Publications.

Vasubandhu, & Anacker, S. (1984). *Seven works of Vasubandhu, the Buddhist psychological doctor.* Delhi: Motilal Banarsidass.

Velmans, M. N., Yujin. (2012). *Introduction to Monist Alternatives to Physicalism.* Journal of Consciousness Studies: Special Issue on Monist Alternatives to Physicalism, 19 (Number 9-10).

Wallace, B. A., Quirolo, L., & Ye śes rdo, r. (2003). *Buddhism with an attitude : the Tibetan seven-point mind-training* (2nd ed.). Ithaca, NY: Snow Lion Publications.

Xuanzang, Vasubandhu, & Wei, T. (1973). *Ch'eng wei-shih lun; the doctrine of mere-consciousness.* Hong Kong,: Ch'eng Wei-shih Lun Publication Committee.

Xuanzang, Vasubandhu, Xuanzang, Vasubandhu, Cook, F. H., & Numata Center for Buddhist Translation and Research. (1999). *Three texts on Consciousness Only : Demonstration of Consciousness Only.* Berkeley, Calif.: Numata Center for Buddhist Translation and Research.

www.ingramcontent.com/pod-product-compliance
Lightning Source LLC
Chambersburg PA
CBHW032111040426
42337CB00040B/193